Drugs

Editor: Danielle Lobban

Volume 444

First published by Independence Educational Publishers

The Studio, High Green

Great Shelford

Cambridge CB22 5EG

England

© Independence 2024

Copyright

This book is sold subject to the condition that it shall not,
by way of trade or otherwise, be lent, resold, hired out or otherwise
circulated in any form of binding or cover other than that in which it
is published without the publisher's prior consent.

Photocopy licence

The material in this book is protected by copyright. However, the
purchaser is free to make multiple copies of particular articles for instructional
purposes for immediate use within the purchasing institution.
Making copies of the entire book is not permitted.

ISBN-13: 978 1 86168 904 7

Printed in Great Britain

Zenith Print Group

Acknowledgements

The publisher is grateful for permission to reproduce the material in this book. While every care has been taken to trace and acknowledge copyright, the publisher tenders its apology for any accidental infringement or where copyright has proved untraceable. The publisher would be pleased to come to a suitable arrangement in any such case with the rightful owner.

The material reproduced in **issues** books is provided as an educational resource only. The views, opinions and information contained within reprinted material in **issues** books do not necessarily represent those of Independence Educational Publishers and its employees.

Images

Cover image courtesy of iStock. All other images courtesy of Freepik, Pixabay, Pexels, and Unsplash. Except page 22: iStock.

Additional acknowledgements

With thanks to the Independence team: Janey Hills, Klaudia Sommer, and Jackie Staines.

Danielle Lobban

Cambridge, May 2024

Contents

Chapter 1: Drug Use and Abuse

Reasons for drug use	1
Why do people take drugs?	2
What are the dangers from using drugs?	3
The effects of drugs on the body	6
New psychoactive substances	10
How many Britons have used recreational drugs?	12
Generation X hardest hit as drug deaths rise yet again in England and Wales	16
Prescription drug addiction	18
Matthew Perry: the tragedy of extreme addiction is that the body may never recover	20
Taking laughing gas 600 times a week left me in a wheelchair	22

Chapter 2: Drugs and The Law

Drugs and the law	23
Drugs penalties	24
Is it time to consider decriminalising drugs in the UK?	26
Has the time come for reform of the UK's drug policy?	28
Should possessing or selling drugs be legal?	30
UK drug policy: how seizing passports will not stop illicit drug use	32
Illegal muscle-building drugs being sold in UK shops, says report	33
Gang jailed for drugs smuggling through the UK and Ireland	34

Chapter 3: Safety & Support

Tips for supporting someone with drug and alcohol problems	35
Peer mentor programmes could become a pathway out of addiction	36
MPs call for magic mushrooms and psychedelic drugs to be downgraded	37
Drug use is a health problem': inside one of the world's oldest legal consumption rooms	38
Feeling pressured to take drugs? Here are 10 ways to deal with it	40
Spiking – how to protect yourself on a night out	41

Further Reading/Useful Websites	42
Glossary	43
Index	44

Introduction

Drugs is Volume 444 in the **issues** series. The aim of the series is to offer current, diverse information about important issues in our world, from a UK perspective.

About *Drugs*

The UK has one of the highest rates of drug-induced deaths in Europe. This book explores the reasons why people take drugs, the risks of abusing both illegal and legal drugs and their impact on mental and physical health.

Our sources

Titles in the **issues** series are designed to function as educational resource books, providing a balanced overview of a specific subject.

The information in our books is comprised of facts, articles and opinions from many different sources, including:

- Newspaper reports and opinion pieces
- Website factsheets
- Magazine and journal articles
- Statistics and surveys
- Government reports
- Literature from special interest groups.

A note on critical evaluation

Because the information reprinted here is from a number of different sources, readers should bear in mind the origin of the text and whether the source is likely to have a particular bias when presenting information (or when conducting their research). It is hoped that, as you read about the many aspects of the issues explored in this book, you will critically evaluate the information presented.

It is important that you decide whether you are being presented with facts or opinions. Does the writer give a biased or unbiased report? If an opinion is being expressed, do you agree with the writer? Is there potential bias to the 'facts' or statistics behind an article?

Activities

Throughout this book, you will find a selection of assignments and activities designed to help you engage with the articles you have been reading and to explore your own opinions. Some tasks will take longer than others and there is a mixture of design, writing and research-based activities that you can complete alone or in a group.

Further research

At the end of each article we have listed its source and a website that you can visit if you would like to conduct your own research. Please remember to critically evaluate any sources that you consult and consider whether the information you are viewing is accurate and unbiased.

Issues Online

The **issues** series of books is complemented by our online resource, issuesonline.co.uk

On the Issues Online website you will find a wealth of information, covering over 70 topics, to support the PSHE and RSE curriculum.

Why Issues Online?

Researching a topic? Issues Online is the best place to start for...

Librarians

Issues Online is an essential tool for librarians: feel confident you are signposting safe, reliable, user-friendly online resources to students and teaching staff alike. We provide multi-user concurrent access, so no waiting around for another student to finish with a resource. Issues Online also provides FREE downloadable posters for your shelf/wall/table displays.

Teachers

Issues Online is an ideal resource for lesson planning, inspiring lively debate in class and setting lessons and homework tasks.

Our accessible, engaging content helps deepen students' knowledge, promotes critical thinking and develops independent learning skills.

Issues Online saves precious preparation time. We wade through the wealth of material on the internet to filter the best quality, most relevant and up-to-date information you need to start exploring a topic.

Our carefully selected, balanced content presents an overview and insight into each topic from a variety of sources and viewpoints.

Students

Issues Online is designed to support your studies in a broad range of topics, particularly social issues relevant to young people today.

There are thousands of articles, statistics and infographs instantly available to help you with research and assignments.

With 24/7 access using the powerful Algolia search system, you can find relevant information quickly, easily and safely anytime from your laptop, tablet or smartphone, in class or at home.

Visit issuesonline.co.uk to find out more!

Chapter 1: Drug Use & Abuse

Reasons for drug use

Drug use is a complex issue that affects people of all ages, genders, races, and backgrounds. You may have seen or heard about people taking drugs on TV, in movies, or even in your community, and might be wondering why someone would choose to do so. In this book, we will explore the different reasons why people take drugs and the potential risks involved.

To begin with, some people take drugs for medicinal purposes. This means that a doctor has prescribed the drug to help them treat a medical condition. For example, someone with asthma might use an inhaler to help them breathe freely. Similarly, someone with ADHD might take medication to help them focus better at school. In these cases, the drugs are used under the supervision of a medical professional and are taken as prescribed.

On the other hand, some people take drugs for recreational purposes. This means that they use drugs to achieve a desired effect or feeling. For instance, some people might take drugs to feel happy, relaxed, or more sociable. Others might take drugs to enhance their performance, such as athletes using steroids to build up muscle mass.

However, recreational drug use can be dangerous, especially if the person takes too much or mixes different drugs together. This can lead to serious health problems, such as addiction, overdose, or even death.

Another reason why people take drugs is peer pressure. This means that they feel pressured to try drugs by their friends or social group. Sometimes, people might feel like they have to take drugs to fit in, be liked, or be seen as 'cool.' However, giving in to peer pressure can be risky. Not only can it lead to serious health problems, but it can also damage relationships and even lead to legal trouble if the person is caught possessing or selling illegal drugs.

Moreover, some people take drugs to cope with stress or emotional pain. This means that they use drugs to numb their feelings or escape from reality. For example, someone who has suffered a traumatic experience might use drugs to avoid thinking about it. Similarly, someone who is going through a difficult time in their life might use drugs to feel better or forget their problems. However, using drugs to cope with emotional pain can be harmful in the long run. It can lead to addiction, mental health problems, and even more stress and pain.

Lastly, some people take drugs out of curiosity or a desire for new experiences. This means that they use drugs to explore different sensations or feelings. For example, someone might try LSD to experience hallucinations, or ecstasy to feel euphoric. However, experimenting with drugs is risky, as the chemicals in the drugs arent controlled, and the person might not know how their body will react to the drug or how much to take. This can lead to unpredictable and dangerous situations.

People take drugs for a variety of reasons, including medicinal purposes, recreational purposes, peer pressure, coping with stress or emotional pain, and curiosity or a desire for new experiences. While some reasons might seem harmless or even beneficial, it's important to understand the potential risks involved with drug use. By arming yourself with knowledge, seeking help if needed, and surrounding yourself with positive influences, you can make healthy and informed choices for your mind and body. Remember, your health and well-being should always come first.

Why do people take drugs?

1. Enjoyment

One of the main reasons people take drugs is because they find it enjoyable to alter their perceptions. They may like the feelings of excitement, confidence, and connection with others, which some drugs can give.

2. Environment

Some people live in communtities which suffer from high unemployment, low-quality housing, and where the infrastructure of local services is poorly resourced. In such communities, drug supply and use can thrive as an alternative economy. As well as use that might be associated with the stress and boredom of living in such communities, people with poor job prospects may recognise the financial advantages of the business of drug supply.

3. Curiosity and experimentation

Many people are naturally curious and want to experiment with different experiences. For some, drugs are a good conversation point.

4. Defence mechanism/self-medicating

Some people use drugs to help them forget about problems, including any traumatic experiences they may have had. Drugs may also be seen as a way to help people relax and deal with stress, or to help deal wtih anxiety, depression, and other mental health problems.

5. Natural rebellion

With young people in particular, taking drugs can be part of natural rebellion. Drug use may act as a means of defiance or may be associated with belonging to an alternative culture.

5. Availablity/medical use/price

Drugs are everywhere. People are often seen smoking and using alcohol on television. People may be prescribed drugs for medical reasons, such as tranquillisers or opioid painkillers, which they become dependent upon. Drugs may now be ordered off the dark web and received at homes by post.

Drugs can be a cheap way of getting a high. Cannabis sufficient for a few joints would cost around £5. In terms of how long the effects last, this compares favourably with an average price for a pint of lager of around £4–5.

7. Peer pressure

There is considerable pressure to use legal substances. Being around others who are using drugs can make people feel like they have to follow suit to fit in. For example, it may be hard to abstain from alcohol in a pub where everyone else is drinking.

The above information is reprinted with kind permission from DrugWise.
© 2024 DrugWise

www.drugwise.org.uk

What are the dangers from using drugs?

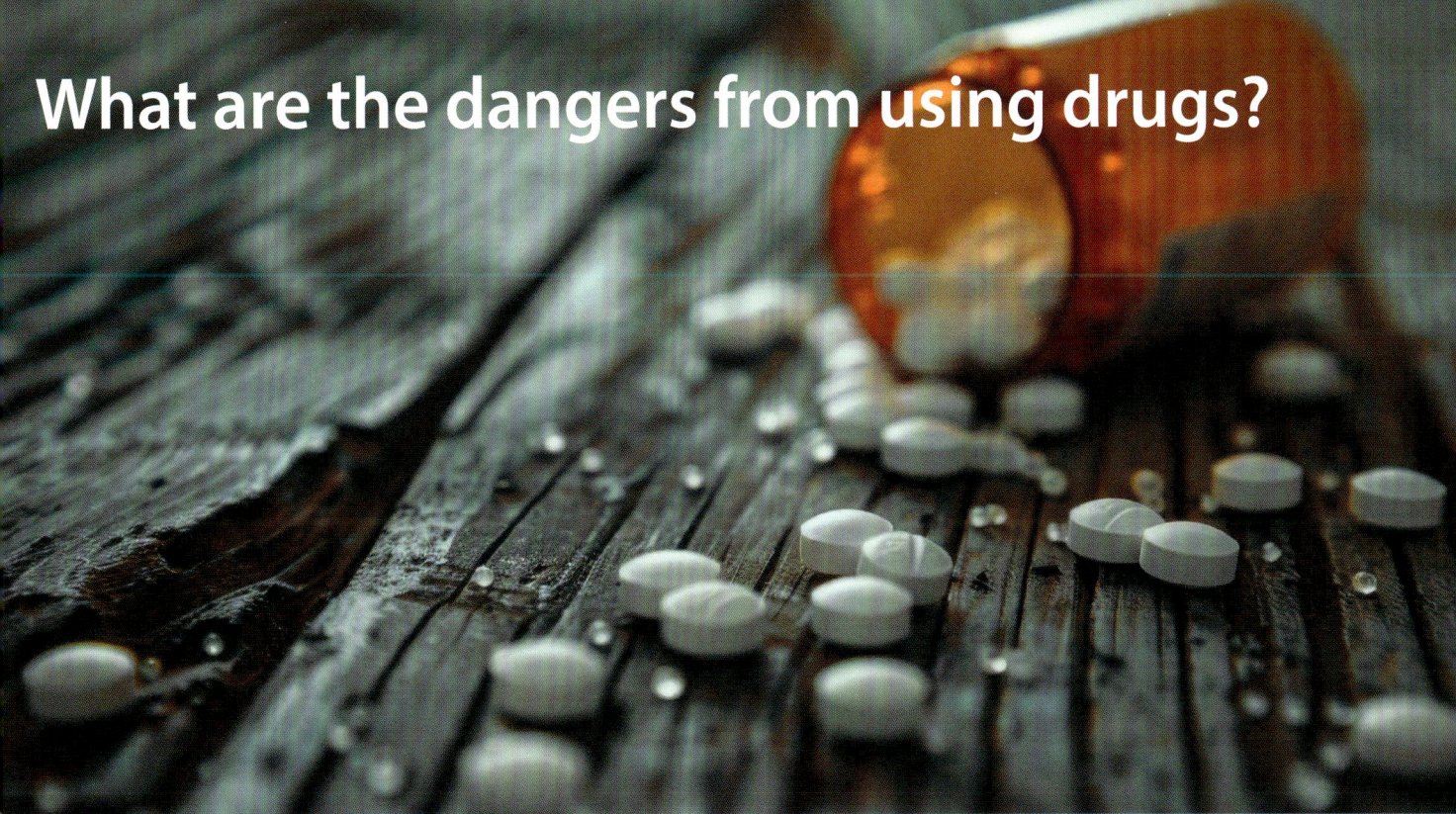

Some people think everyone who takes drugs will end up dead. Others seem to think that drug use is not dangerous at all. The truth is somewhere in between…

Drug use can never be 100% safe but it is not always as dangerous as people think. The dangers of drug use depend on drug, set, and setting factors.

The 'drug' part is everything connected with the drug and how it is used. The 'set' part is everything connected with the person who is using the drugs. The 'setting' part is about what the person is doing at the time, where they are, the environment they live in, and so on.

The basic principle is that drug dangers are the result of interactions between drug, set and setting.

The drug

Drugs are not all the same and different drugs have different dangers associated with them.

Some drugs (such as alcohol, heroin and tranquillisers) have a sedative effect which slow down the way the body and brain function. They can have a numbing effect that produces drowsiness if a lot is taken.

Other drugs (such as amphetamine, cocaine, crack and ecstasy) have a stimulant effect giving a rush of energy and making people more alert.

A third group of drugs (such as LSD and magic mushrooms, and to a lesser extent cannabis and ecstasy) have a hallucinogenic effect. This means they tend to alter the way the user feels, sees, hears, tastes or smells.

Sedative drugs like alcohol and heroin can lead to fatal overdose if a lot is taken. They can also affect coordination, making accidents more likely. Use of sedatives can also lead to physical dependence and withdrawal symptoms while other drugs like cannabis cannot.

Stimulant drugs can produce anxiety or panic attacks, particularly if taken in large quantities. They can be particularly dangerous for people who have heart or blood pressure problems.

Hallucinogenic drugs sometimes produce very disturbing experiences and may lead to erratic or dangerous behaviour by the user.

And of course some drugs are legal to use and others are not. Being arrested and getting a conviction can lead to all sorts of problems.

The dangers of drug use will also depend on:

- How much is taken. The more that is taken the greater the danger. Taking too much of a sedative drug can lead to a fatal overdose. Taking a large dose of a stimulant drug can lead to panic attacks, heart problems, or, in extreme cases, psychotic behaviour (where all sense of reality is lost). Taking a large dose of a hallucinogenic drug may lead to disturbing experiences. Taking a high dose of many drugs can lead to a lack of coordination and increase the likelihood of accidents.

- How often the drug is taken. The more often a drug is taken, the greater the risks to your health, particularly if the body hasn't had time to recover. With some drugs a tolerance can develop and more needs to be taken in order to keep getting an effect. If heavy, frequent use is followed by a period of non-use, tolerance levels drop. Taking the same amount of drug needed with high tolerance levels can bring on an overdose, especially with drugs like heroin. Not all drugs produce tolerance. LSD has its own safeguard against tolerance: if taken too frequently it just stops working and no matter how much is taken there will be no effect at all.

- Other things in drugs. Many illegal drugs, especially in powder or pill form, have other drugs or substances mixed in with them. These can change the effect of the drugs and contribute to dangers.

- Drug mixtures. Combining drugs can produce unpredictable and sometimes dangerous effects. In particular, mixtures of sedative drugs can be very dangerous. Many reported drug overdoses involve mixtures of alcohol and tranquillisers or opiates.

- How a drug is taken. The method of use will influence the effect the drug has and its possible dangers. See section below for more information.

As mentioned, drug dangers also vary with the method used to take them:

- Injecting drugs has a very quick and intense effect, it is particularly risky because it is difficult to know how much is being taken. Injection also carries the risk of infection by blood-borne diseases if any injecting equipment is shared. Highest profile recently has been given to HIV, the virus that leads to AIDS, but there are also risks from hepatitis B and C, which are also very serious blood-borne viruses.

- Eating or drinking a drug is the method with the slowest effect but it can be risky if people take a lot in one go. The effects tend to be slow but once they come on it is too late to do anything about it. Examples are drinking too much alcohol in a short space of time or eating a lump of cannabis. In such cases people can suddenly feel very drunk or stoned and become very disorientated.

- Snorting is another quick and intense method (though not as much as injecting). Snorting drugs like amphetamine or cocaine powder up the nose on a regular basis can lead to damage to the nasal membranes although this risk has sometimes been exaggerated.

There are more and less dangerous ways of inhaling solvents such as glues, gases, and aerosols. Squirting solvents into a large plastic bag and then placing the bag over the head has led to death by suffocation. Squirting aerosols or

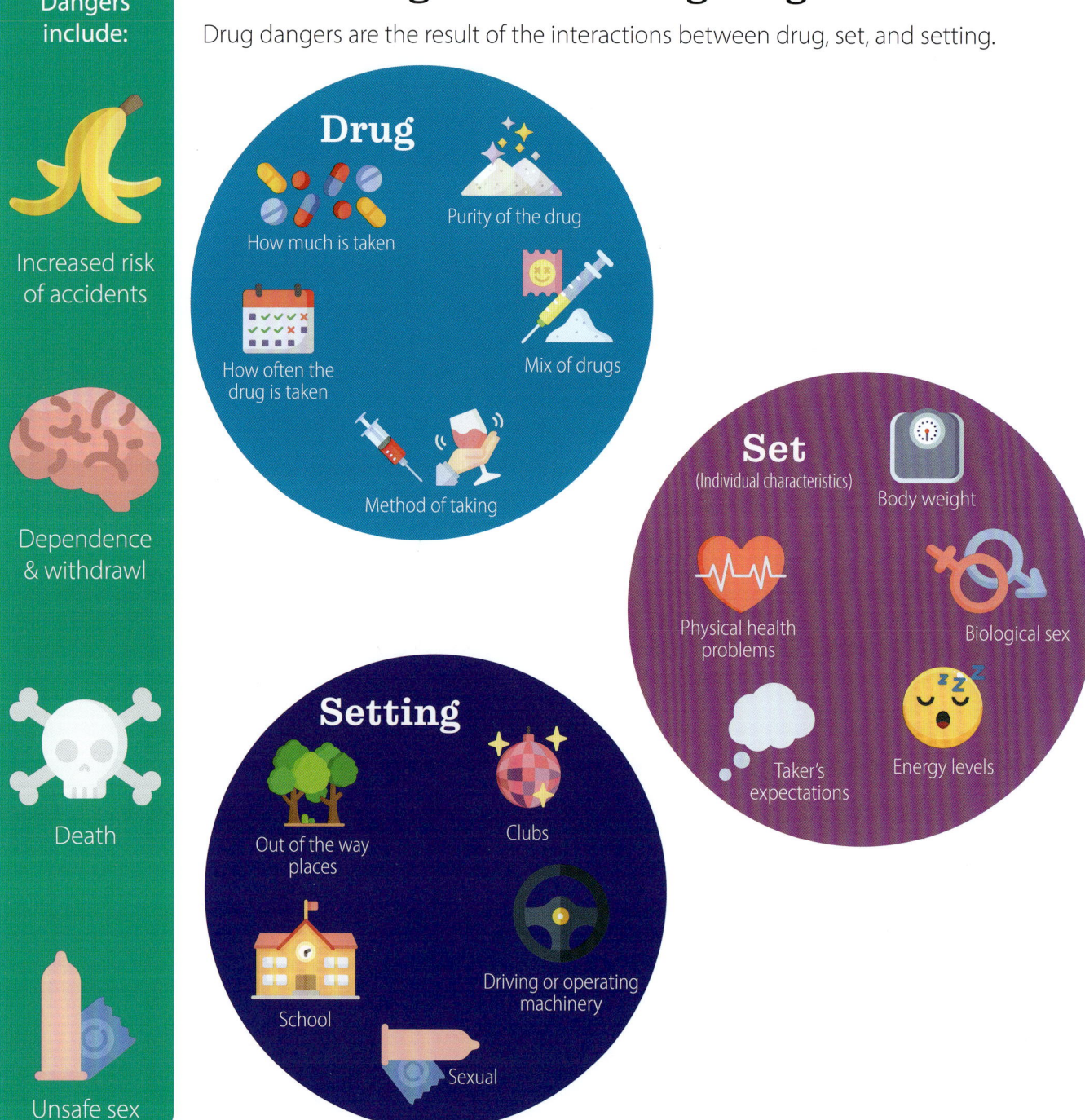

Source: DrugWise

butane straight down the throat has led to deaths through freezing of the airways. Squirting onto a rag or small bag then inhaling is not as dangerous as the previous methods, however, it still carries risks.

Smoking a drug is a relatively less dangerous method of use although regular smoking can damage the respiratory system especially if the drug is smoked with tobacco, as is often the case with cannabis.

The set

The effects and dangers of drugs are influenced by many things. Personal factors involving the person who is using the drugs can be just as important as the drugs being used.

The drug experience and the expectations of the user are important. Many young people experimenting with drugs for the first time will be unsure about what to do or what to expect. This ignorance and lack of experience can itself be dangerous.

The mental or psychological state of the drug user is very important. The mood people are in when they take drugs influences the effects and dangers of drug use. If they are anxious, depressed, or unstable they are more likely to have disturbing experiences when using drugs. They can become more anxious and disorientated, possibly aggressive, 'freak out' and do crazy things, or take too much, and so on. As a general rule someone who is happy and stable is more likely to use more carefully and not be so badly affected.

Other things about the person which may affect drug dangers include:

- If they have physical health problems like heart disease, high blood pressure, epilepsy, diabetes, asthma, or liver problems, drug use could be more dangerous and possibly make their health problem worse.
- The drug user's energy levels at the time of consuming drugs can also be important. If they are tired at the time of use then it may have a different or more extreme effect than if they are fresh and full of energy.
- If the user has a low body weight, the same amount of drugs may affect them more than heavier people. Also people who have eating disorders like anorexia or bulimia can find that drug use makes their eating difficulties even worse.
- Males and females can experience drugs in different ways. This is both because of their different physical make-up and the different way people view male and female drug use. On average, women are of smaller body weight than men, have smaller livers as a proportion of body weight, and have a greater proportion of body fat. This means that, generally speaking, the same amount of drugs will have a greater effect on a woman than on a man. Obviously this will not apply with a much larger than average woman or a much smaller than average man. The effects and risks of drug use are also influenced by attitudes towards men and women taking drugs. Male drug use is often seen as more acceptable than that of women. Mothers in particular come in for a lot of criticism if they use drugs. Male drug users who are parents are not usually seen in the same way.

The setting

The place where drugs are used and what people are doing at the time can influence how dangerous they are. For example, some young people take drugs in out-of-the-way places that are particularly dangerous, like canal banks, near motorways, in derelict buildings, and so on. Accidents are much more likely in these places, especially if the user is intoxicated. Also if anything does go wrong, it is unlikely help will be at hand or that an ambulance could easily be called.

Even if the setting is not in itself inherently dangerous there may be other types of risks associated with the place of use. Using drugs at, or taking drugs into school has led to substantial numbers of young people being expelled from school with drastic effects on their future careers.

Driving a car, riding a bicycle, or operating machinery while on drugs will greatly increase the risks of accidents.

Drug use can lower inhibitions, increasing the likelihood of sexual encounters. Safer sex – for example, by using condoms – will be much more difficult if the person concerned is intoxicated. The risks of unwanted pregnancy, HIV (the virus that leads to AIDS), and other sexually transmitted infections could be increased if people have sex while high on alcohol or drugs. Surveys have found that many young people have sexual encounters while under the influence of drugs, particularly alcohol and/or cannabis.

Another setting danger is that of people over-exerting themselves when using ecstasy. Ecstasy gives a buzz of energy and is often used in clubs while dancing non-stop for long periods. In some situations people have danced for hours without a break in hot, crowded environments. They run the risk of becoming dehydrated and getting heat exhaustion. In some cases this can be very dangerous and it has led to a number of deaths.

In conclusion

There are many possible risks and dangers involved when using drugs. To fully understand potential risks and dangers you will need to think about the drug, set, and setting.

In addition, people may experience problems with drug use because of other people's perceptions and responses to them. Examples include conflict in family and other personal relationships, getting thrown out of school/college or work, getting a criminal record, getting into debt to pay for drugs, violence associated with drug dealing, and so on.

December 2022

Mindmap

Create a mindmap with the risks of drug-taking.

The above information is reprinted with kind permission from DrugWise.
© 2024 DrugWise

www.drugwise.org.uk

The effects of drugs on the body

The type of drug you choose to take can have a significant impact on your body. There are three main drug classifications – stimulants, depressants, and hallucinogens – and each one can produce different effects.

Stimulants are drugs that increase brain and body activity. They work by enhancing the effects of neurotransmitters, primarily dopamine and norepinephrine. This can create feelings of alertness, energy, and even euphoria. Some common types of stimulants include caffeine, nicotine, and amphetamines. While these substances can provide a temporary boost, they can also be addictive and have long-term effects on the body. Over time, stimulant use can lead to insomnia, anxiety, and even heart and blood pressure problems.

Depressants, on the other hand, are substances that slow down the body's functioning. They primarily function by increasing the effects of the neurotransmitter gamma-aminobutyric acid (GABA), which can create feelings of relaxation and calmness. Alcohol, benzodiazepines, and barbiturates are all depressants that are commonly abused. While these substances can produce initial feelings of calmness and relaxation, they can also lead to respiratory problems, coma, and even death in large enough doses.

Hallucinogens, also known as psychedelics, are drugs that distort perception and create altered states of consciousness. These substances can produce vivid visual hallucinations, increased self-awareness, and altered sensory experiences. Some examples of hallucinogens include LSD, mescaline, and psilocybin mushrooms. While these substances are not typically physically addictive, they can lead to anxiety, panic attacks, and even psychotic episodes in some individuals.

How drugs affect people differently

When it comes to illegal drugs, it's crucial to understand that everyone's body reacts differently. What might seem like a fun time to one person can turn into a nightmare for someone else. It's a bit like playing a dangerous game of chance, where the results can be unpredictable and, at times, devastating.

Firstly, drugs can mess with your brain chemistry. They can trick your brain into releasing large amounts of 'feel good' chemicals like dopamine. Sounds fun, right? But here's the catch: over time, your brain might demand the drug to just feel normal, leading to addiction. And the way this process happens can vary wildly from one person to another. While one person might try a drug and not feel compelled to take it again, another might quickly find themselves unable to stop.

Moreover, physical reactions can also differ. Some might experience an intense high or euphoria, while others could have terrifying hallucinations or even physical symptoms like vomiting, increased heart rate, or worse. Factors like your body's chemistry, the presence of other substances in your system, and even your mood at the time can influence how you react to a drug.

Lastly, illegal drugs come with zero quality control. There's no way to be sure of what you're actually taking. One batch might be much stronger than another, or it might be mixed with harmful substances. This unpredictability adds another layer of risk.

In a nutshell, dabbling with illegal drugs is like rolling the dice with your health and well-being. You can never predict how your body will react, and the consequences can sometimes be irreversible. So, before considering going down that path, think about whether it's worth the gamble.

Feeling high or feeling low: the short-term effects of illegal drugs

Ever wonder what happens to your body when you're under the influence of drugs? Let's take a look at how these substances affect us in the short term.

1. **Brain on blast:** When you use drugs, your brain gets hit with chemicals that can make you feel pleasure or a 'high.' Sounds cool? Not quite. This artificial buzz can mess with your ability to make decisions, remember stuff, and even control your emotions. It's like your brain's natural wiring gets all tangled up.

2. **Heart races and risks:** Stimulants, like cocaine or ecstasy, can make your heart race like you've just sprinted a mile. Sure, that might sound like no biggie, but it's super stressful for your heart and can even lead to serious stuff like a heart attack – not so cool for someone just looking to have fun.

3. **Breathe or not:** Some drugs slow down your breathing, which can be super dangerous. If you take too much (and it's easy to do), you might not get enough oxygen, which can lead to passing out or even worse.

4. **Sick to your stomach:** This isn't just about feeling queasy. Drugs can actually make you throw up or feel super sick. In addition, they can affect your appetite – some make you eat more than usual, while others cause a loss of appetite.

Long-term effects of illegal drugs on your body

Taking illegal drugs, even just trying them out, can lead to long-term harm to your body. Every choice we make about our health sets us up for the future, so it's vital to know the stakes. Here are some ways illegal drugs can impact your body over time:

- **Brain damage:** Many drugs, like marijuana, heroin, and methamphetamines, can alter how your brain functions. The damage can result in memory loss, difficulty in learning, and emotional problems like anxiety and depression that might stick with you for a long time.

- **Heart issues:** Your heart doesn't escape the reach of drugs either. Cocaine, amphetamines, and ecstasy can cause long-lasting heart damage, leading to heart attacks or strokes, even in young people.

- **Liver damage:** Drugs like inhalants and anabolic steroids can severely damage your liver, the organ that helps clean toxins out of your body. This can lead to life-threatening conditions like liver failure.

- **Addiction:** Most illegal drugs are highly addictive. Over time, your body and brain might start depending on these drugs to feel normal. Fighting addiction is difficult and impacts your mental, emotional, and physical health.

- **Respiratory problems:** Smoking drugs such as marijuana or crack cocaine damages your lungs and can lead to chronic issues like bronchitis or lung infections. These problems might not show up immediately but can seriously affect your life quality later on.

Drugs affect the way you:

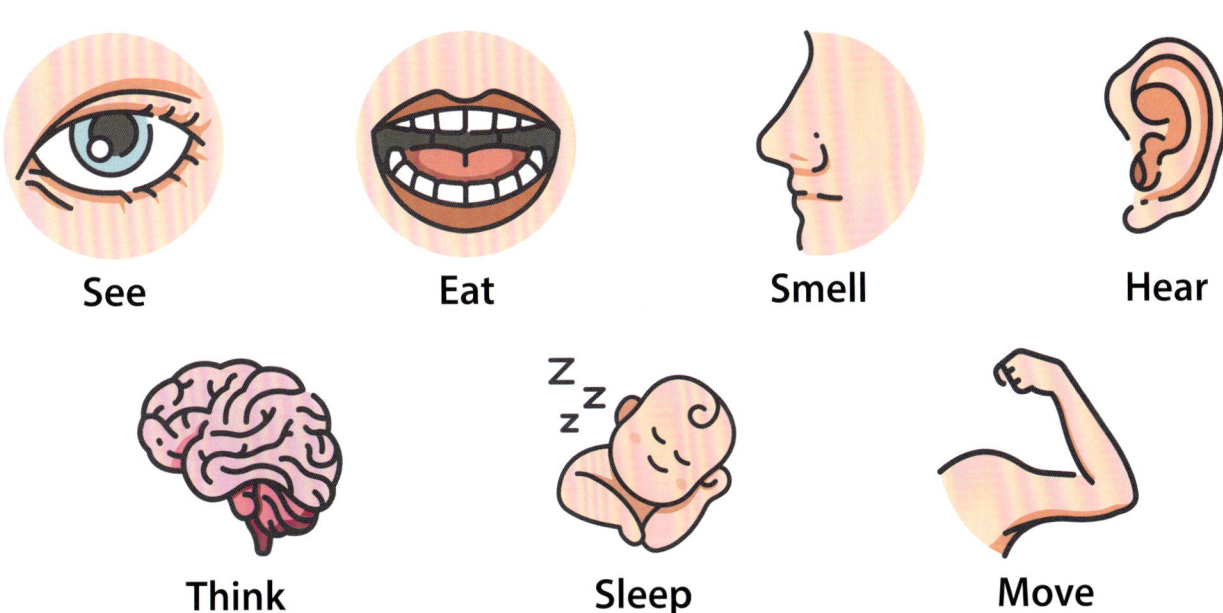

See   Eat   Smell   Hear

Think   Sleep   Move

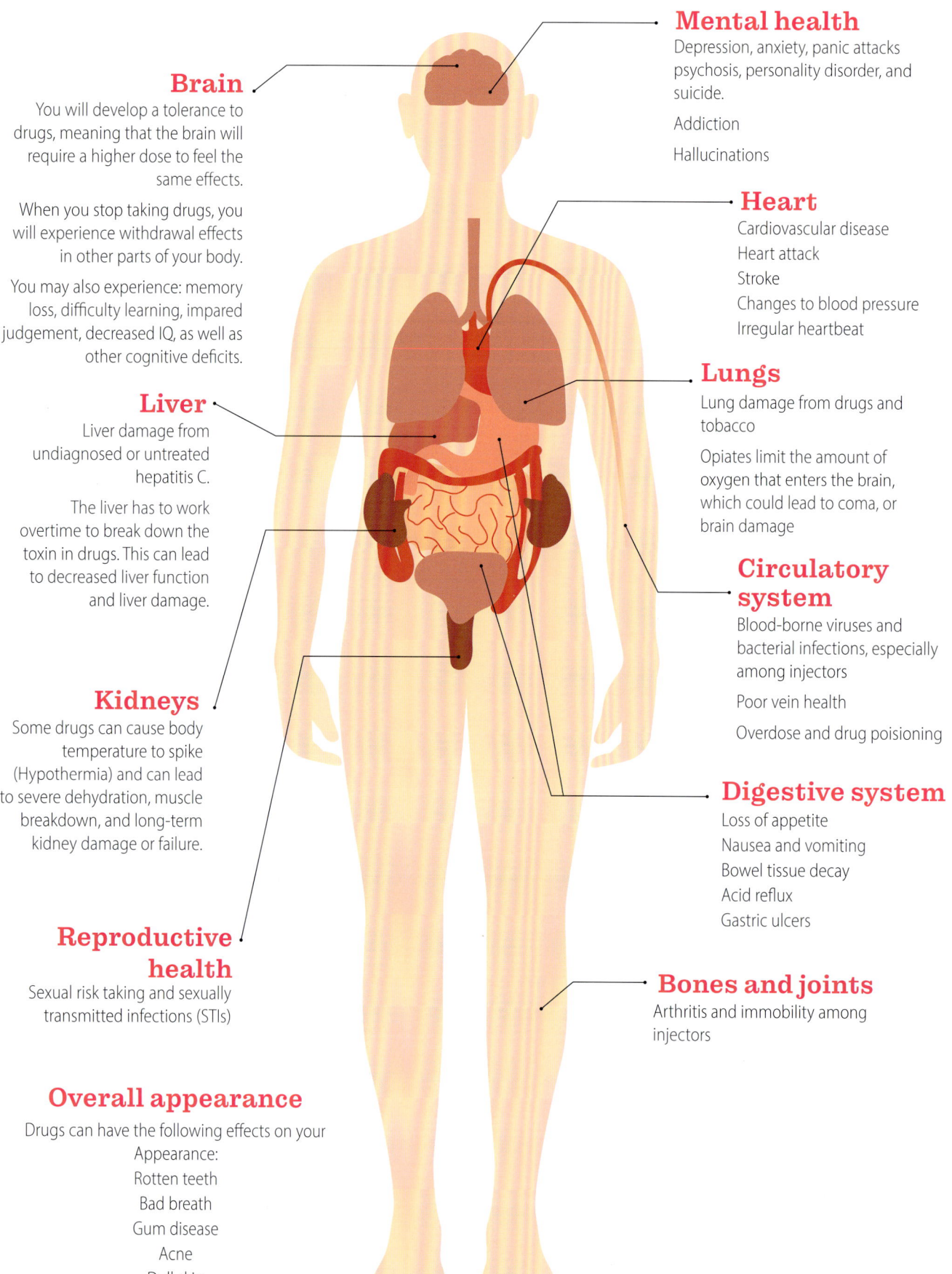

Effects of drugs on mental health

Navigating the maze of mental health is tricky at the best of times, and it gets even more complicated when illegal drugs come into play. Understanding how these substances intertwine with our mental well-being can be a bit like piecing together a puzzle without seeing the picture on the box. Let's dive in and decode how illegal drugs can impact mental health, making the complex a bit more manageable.

Picture this: Your brain is a super-busy communication hub, constantly sending and receiving messages to keep things running smoothly. Now, imagine introducing illegal drugs into this mix. These substances can hijack the natural process, sometimes speeding messages up or slowing them down, leading to a range of mental health effects that can be as unpredictable as British weather.

For starters, certain drugs can serve up a cocktail of anxiety and depression, leaving the user in a mental fog. Others might whisk you away on a thrill ride of euphoria, only to drop you off in a valley of paranoia and distress. The aftermath? A brain trying to recalibrate its natural equilibrium, often struggling with the shadows of addiction, mood swings, and altered perceptions.

Withdrawal

When someone decides to stop using illegal drugs after repeated use, their body can undergo a significant and often challenging process known as withdrawal. Let's delve into this complex journey, breaking down the effects on the body with clear, accessible insights.

Imagine your body as a machine that's been running on a certain fuel for so long that it's become accustomed to operating with that substance. Suddenly removing this substance is akin to throwing a wrench in the works; the body needs to readjust and recalibrate its systems. Withdrawal effects can vary widely, depending largely on the type of drug, the duration of use, and the individual's physical health.

Common physical symptoms of withdrawal may include intense cravings for the drug, sweating, shaking, fatigue, and disturbances in sleep patterns. More severe cases can manifest as heart palpitations, muscle pain, and even seizures. While this sounds daunting, understanding these effects is a crucial step in addressing drug addiction responsibly and seeking support.

But it's not just physical. Emotional and psychological symptoms, such as anxiety, irritability, depression, and difficulty concentrating, can also surface, making everyday tasks and interactions feel overwhelmingly challenging.

However, with the right kind of support – whether from healthcare professionals or family members – people can navigate through withdrawal and move towards recovery.

Design

Design a poster with either the long- or short-term effects of drugs on your body.

New psychoactive substances

Designer drugs, legal highs, new psychoactive substances (NPS), research chemicals.

What are new psychoactive substances?

New psychoactive substances (NPS) are drugs which were designed to replicate the effects of illegal substances like cannabis, cocaine, and ecstasy whilst remaining legal – hence their previous name 'legal highs'.

NPS began to appear in the UK drug scene around 2008/2009. They fall into four main categories:

Synthetic cannabinoids – these drugs mimic cannabis and are traded under such names as Clockwork Orange, Black Mamba, Spice and Exodus Damnation. They bear no relation to the cannabis plant except that the chemicals which are blended into the base plant matter act on the brain in a similar way to cannabis.

Stimulant-type drugs – these drugs mimic substances such as amphetamine, cocaine and ecstasy and include benzylpiperazine (BZP), mephedrone, methylenedioxypyrovalerone (MDPV) naphyrone (NRG-1), Benzo Fury, methylenedioxy-2-aminoindane (MDAI), and ethylphenidate.

'Downer'/tranquiliser-type drugs – these drugs mimic tranquiliser or anti-anxiety drugs, in particular from the benzodiazepine family and include Etizolam, Pyrazolam and Flubromazepam.

Hallucinogenic drugs – these drugs mimic substances like LSD and include 25i-NBOMe, Bromo-Dragonfly, and the more ketamine-like methoxetamine.

NPS are sold online and in shops (although they were banned in 2016). The drugs come in brightly coloured packaging under a variety of brand names. The packaging may describe a list of ingredients but it's impossible to be sure what's inside and the contents of one branded package could change from week to week.

Effects

The effects of NPS vary significantly from drug to drug and, compared to more traditional drugs, we have relatively little information on them. However, there is a growing body of evidence to demonstrate the potential short- and long-term harms associated with their use. There have been hospitalisations and deaths linked to NPS.

Reported harms during intoxication and come down include:

- Overdose and temporary psychotic states and unpredictable behaviours;
- Attendance at A&E and some hospital admissions;
- Sudden increase in body temperature, heart rate, coma and risk to internal organs;
- Hallucination and vomiting;
- Confusion leading to aggression and violence;
- Intense comedown that can cause users to feel suicidal.

Use was also associated with longer-term health issues:

- Increase in mental health issues including psychosis, paranoia, anxiety, and 'psychiatric complications';
- Depression;
- Physical and psychological dependency happening quite rapidly after a relatively short intense period of use (weeks).

In the Office for National Statistics (ONS) report *Deaths Related to Drug Poisoning in England and Wales: 2019 Registrations*, it states that there were 125 deaths involving new psychoactive substances in 2019 with synthetic cannabinoids being the most frequently mentioned NPS, contributing to 56 deaths.

Xylazine, a drug found in North America as a heroin/fentanyl adulterant, recently had its first associated death reported in the UK. The drug is a veterinary medicine with sedative, analgesic, and muscle-relaxant properties.

The law

While many of these drugs were once legal, with the advent of the Psychoactive Substances Act it is now illegal to produce, supply, or import them for human consumption – including for personal use. Possession for personal use is not an offence, unless in prison.

The Psychoactive Substances Act received Royal Assent on 28 January 2016 and came into force on 26 May 2016.

The act:

- Makes it an offence to produce, supply, offer to supply, possess with intent to supply, possess on custodial premises, import or export psychoactive substances; that is, any substance intended for human consumption that is capable of producing a psychoactive effect. The maximum sentence will be 7 years' imprisonment

- Excludes legitimate substances, such as food, alcohol, tobacco, nicotine, caffeine and medical products

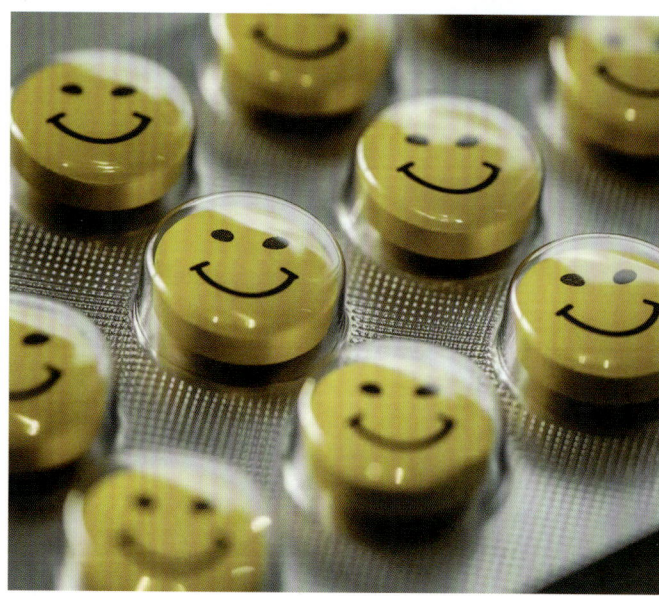

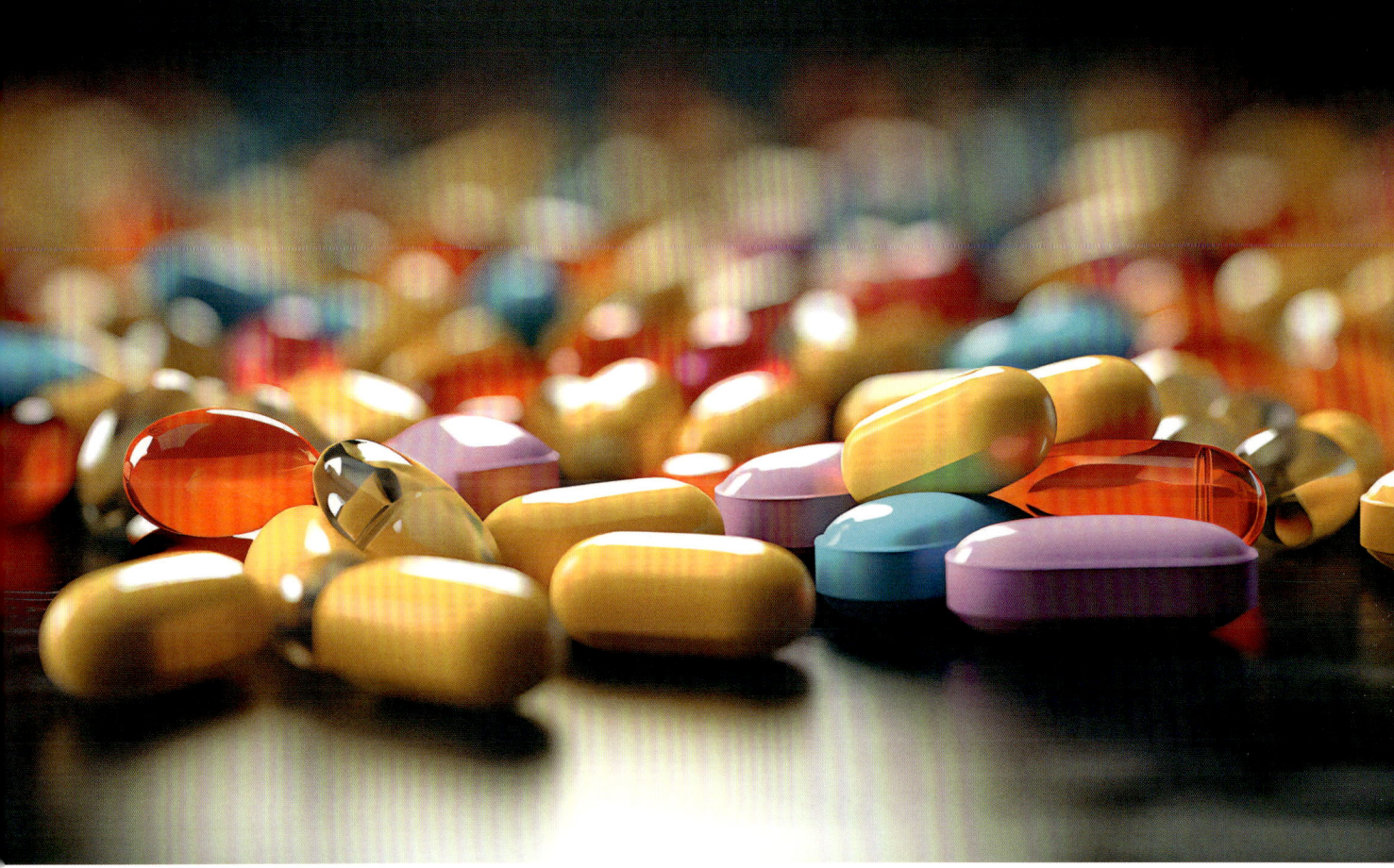

- from the scope of the offence, as well as 'poppers' and controlled drugs, which continue to be regulated by the Misuse of Drugs Act 1971
- Exempts healthcare activities and approved scientific research from the offences under the act on the basis that persons engaged in such activities have a legitimate need to use psychoactive substances in their work
- Includes provision for civil sanctions – prohibition notices, premises notices, prohibition orders and premises orders (breach of the 2 orders will be a criminal offence) – to enable the police and local authorities to adopt a graded response to the supply of psychoactive substances in appropriate cases
- Provides powers to stop and search persons, vehicles and vessels, enter and search premises in accordance with a warrant, and to seize and destroy psychoactive substances

In November 2018 the Home Office published a review of the act that sought to measure changes in outcomes before and after its implementation and thereby provide an indication of whether its aims are being achieved. The review concluded that:

- The open sale of NPS were largely eliminated
- There was a significant fall in NPS use in the general population
- There was a reduction in health-related harms (likely to have been achieved through reduced usage)

However, there was still concern over the supply of NPS by street dealers, the continued development of new substances, the potential displacement from NPS to other harmful substances, and continued high levels of synthetic cannabinoid use among the homeless and prison populations. A study published in 2021 reviewed the effects of the act and concluded that the number of deaths following NPS use has risen despite introduction of the act.

Some synthetic cannabinoids like Spice are controlled as Class B substances under the Misuse of Drugs Act. Offences for Class B drugs are:

- Possession – maximum sentence – five years/fine/both
- Possession with intent to supply – maximum sentence – 14 years/fine/both
- Supply (including being concerned in supply, conspiracy to supply, aggravated supply and offer to supply) – maximum sentence – 14 years/fine/both
- Production – maximum sentence – 14 years/fine/both

However, maximum sentences are rarely used.

Prevalence

According to a report from the Office for National Statistics, *Drug Misuse in England and Wales: Year Ending June 2022*, the level of NPS use in the last year among adults aged 16 to 59 years was 0.4%, and 0.9% for those aged 16 to 24 years. This showed no change compared with the previous report, for the year ending March 2020.

July 2023

The above information is reprinted with kind permission from DrugWise.
© 2024 DrugWise

www.drugwise.org.uk

How many Britons have used recreational drugs?

The YouGov Big Survey on Drugs shows half of Britons (50%) say they know a lot (9%) or something (41%) about recreational drugs, while 38% say they don't know much, and one in ten (10%) don't know anything at all.

Men (13%) are twice as likely as women (6%) to say they 'know a lot' about drugs, with this being the case across all age groups.

Britons aged 60 and older are less likely to say they have at least some knowledge on the subject (41%) compared to other age groups (50–57%).

For the purposes of this study, 'soft drugs' refers to substances like cannabis or speed, and 'hard drugs' refers to substances like cocaine or heroin.

Overall, four in ten Britons (39%) say they have taken recreational drugs, with more than twice as many having taken soft drugs (38%) than hard drugs (14%). Slightly more men (42%) than women (35%) have taken drugs recreationally. Half of Britons between the ages of 25 and 59 say they have taken recreational drugs (49-52%), twice as many as those aged 16–24-year-olds (26%) and 60 or older (24%).

Six in ten Britons (58%) say they have never taken any recreational drugs.

When it comes to soft drugs (such as cannabis or speed), 15% of Britons say they have taken drugs in this category 'many times' and a further 23% have done so 'once or twice'. One in five men (19%) say they have taken soft drugs many times, while this applies to 11% of women.

Among the youngest Britons (16–24), 10% say they have taken soft drugs 'many times' and a further 16% say they've done so 'once or twice'. Among those between the ages of 25 and 59, 49–51% say they have taken soft drugs, falling to one in four (24%) among the 60+ generation.

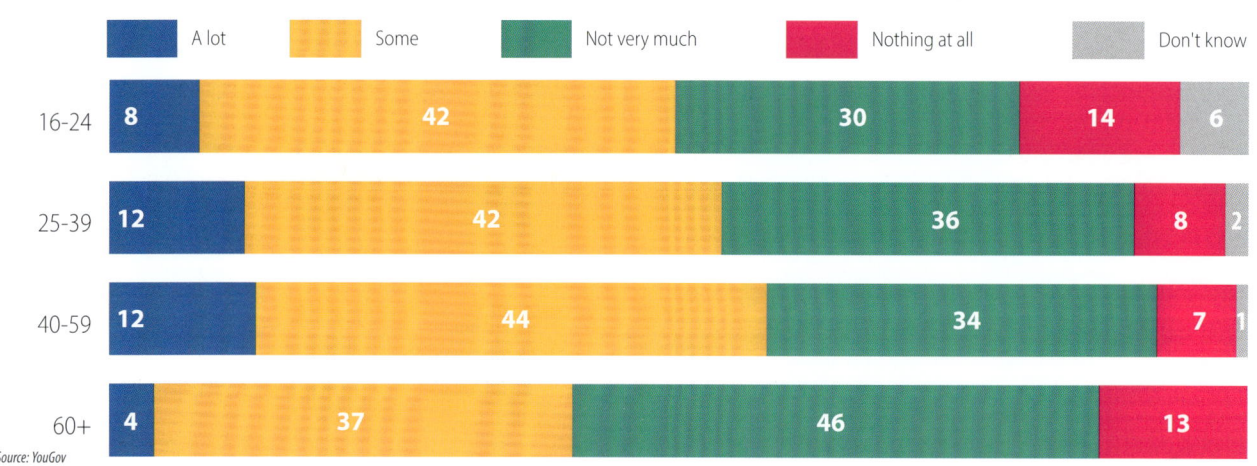

Britons under 60 are more likely to say they know a lot about recreational drugs

How much, if at all, would you say you know about recreational drugs? %

Source: YouGov

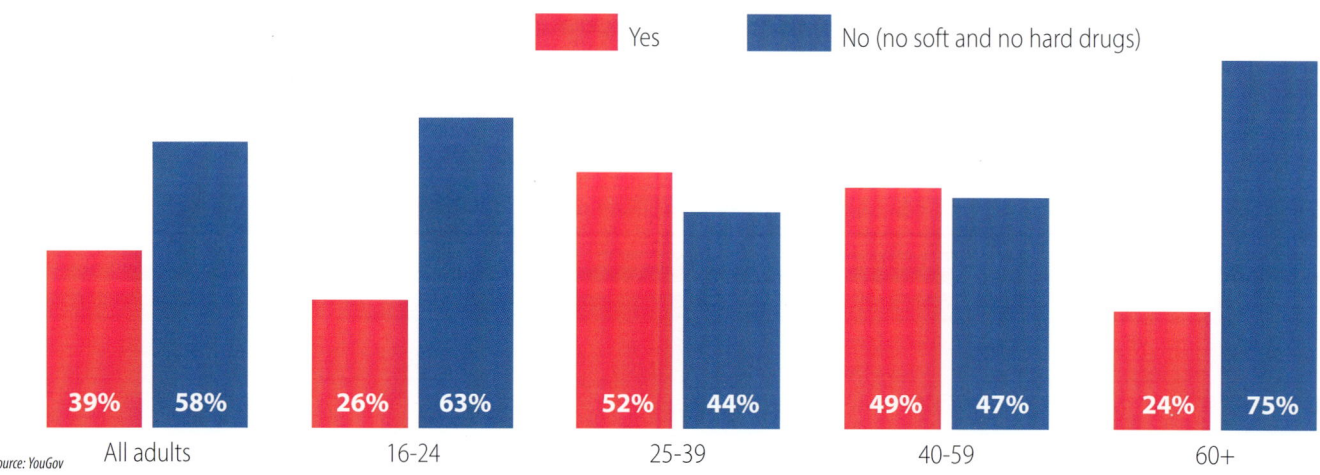

Six in ten Britons have never taken any kind of recreational drug

Have you ever taken any [soft drugs (for example, cannabis or speed)]/[hard drugs (for example, cocaine or heroin)]? %

Source: YouGov

Britons between 25 and 59 are more likely to say they have tried soft drugs

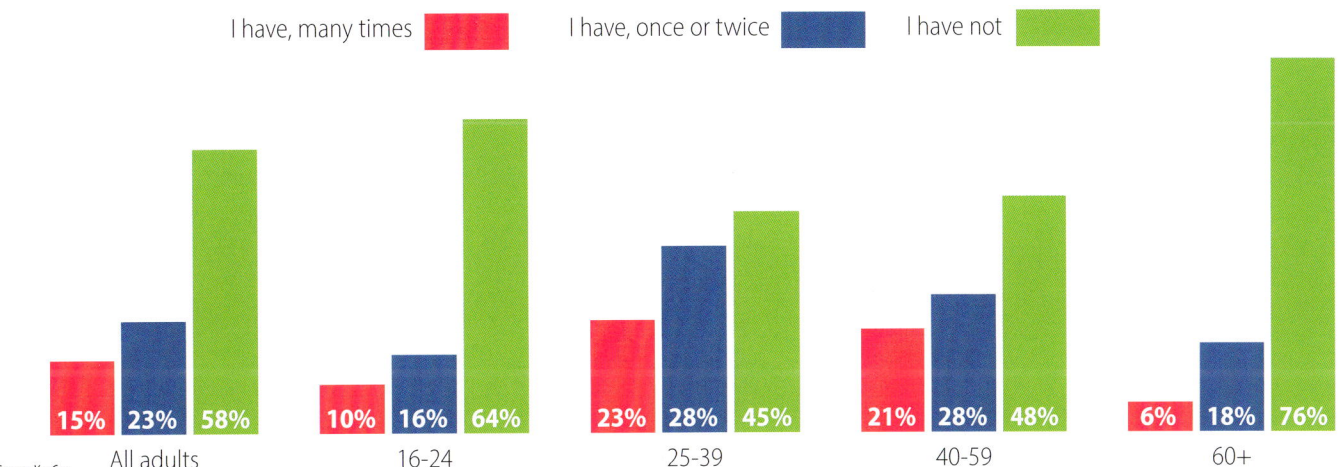

Source: YouGov

Six in ten Britons (58%) say they have never taken soft drugs.

When it comes to using hard drugs (such as cocaine or heroin), 14% of Britons say they have tried them, with 5% saying they have taken hard drugs 'many times,' and 9% saying they've taken them 'once or twice.' Men are twice as likely as women to have tried hard drugs: 19% vs 10%.

Among the youngest Britons (16–24) 14% say they've tried hard drugs, with this climbing to one in four (24%) among those aged 25–t39. Significantly fewer Britons aged 40–59 (16%) or 60 and older (5%) have experimented with hard drugs.

Overall, eight in ten Britons (83%) have never tried hard drugs.

Which recreational drugs have Britons tried?

The following questions were asked only to Britons who said they have taken recreational drugs (39%).

Among Britons who have said they have tried recreational drugs, one in five (21%) say they still take them, with 5% saying they do so often and 16% occasionally. This mostly applies to Britons in the 25–39 age group (26%), falling to 16% among those in their 40s and 50s, and to one in ten (10%) among those 60 or older.

Nine out of ten (93%) Britons who say they have had experience with drugs, have tried cannabis. Cocaine is second (34%), while ecstasy comes third (27%), followed by MDMA (24%), amphetamines (23%) and hashish (23%).

There is a generational split between 25–39-years-olds and the over-40s on which types of drugs they have tried: cocaine (43% vs 34%) and MDMA (37% vs 21%) are more popular among the younger group, while hashish (28% vs 20%) and LSD (24% vs 14%) are more widely experienced among those in their 40s and 50s.

Cannabis is often described as the gateway drug and is the most commonly used illegal drug. Our research shows that among Britons who say they took cannabis and at least one other drug, 83% of them report that cannabis was the first drug they tried, while 14% say they tried other drugs first, before taking cannabis.

One in five Britons (18%) say they have at some point felt pressured by their peers to take recreational drugs, including 7% who caved in and took drugs because of that pressure.

The vast majority of Britons have never tried hard drugs like cocaine or heroin

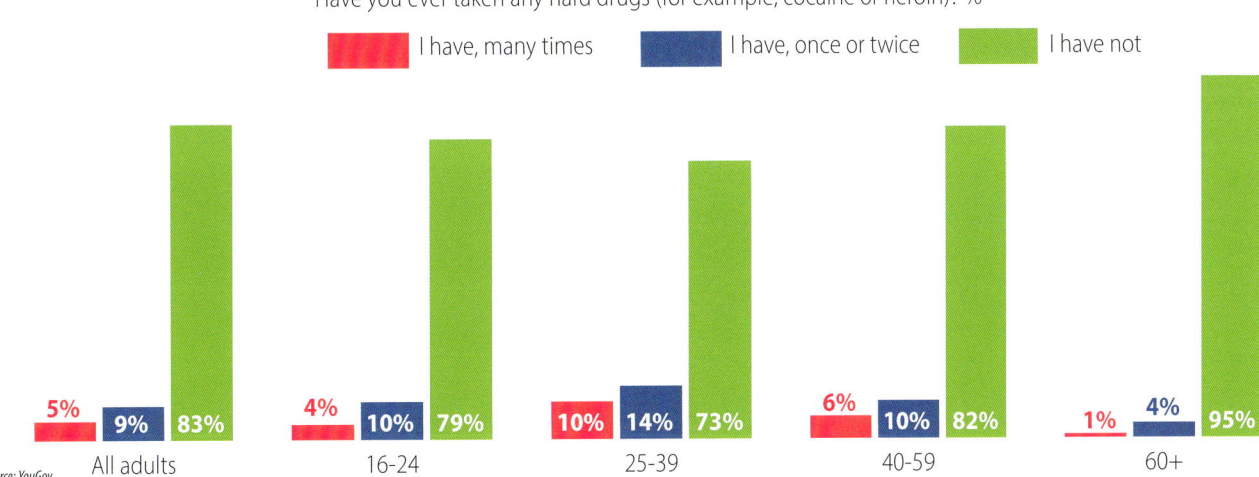

Source: YouGov

issues: Drugs 13 Chapter 1: Drug Use and Abuse

Most Britons who say they have ever taken recreational drugs no longer take them, but one in five still do

Earlier you said you have taken recreational drugs. Do you still take recreational drugs?
% of 1052 Britons who said they had taken recreational drugs

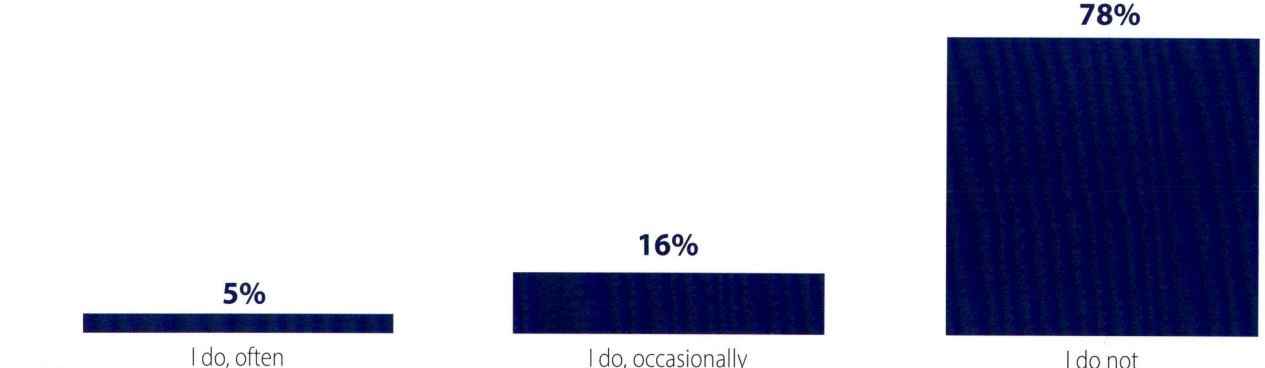

Source: YouGov

For Britons who have had experience with recreational drugs, nine out of ten have tried cannabis

Which of the following drugs have you tried?
% of 1052 Britons who said they had taken recreational drugs

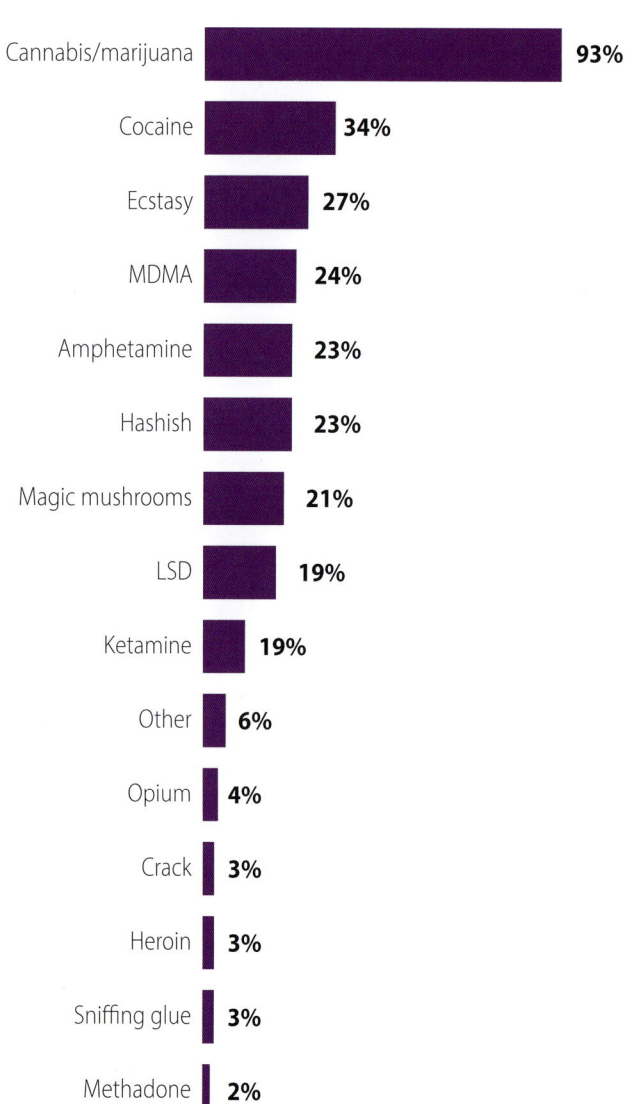

Source: YouGov

One in five (22%) 16–24-year-olds and 28% of 25–39-year-olds report they have felt pressured by their peers to take drugs. This includes 7% and 12% of each group respectively who say they have ended up taking drugs.

Eight in ten (80%) Britons say they have never felt any peer pressure to take recreational drugs.

Half of Britons (51%) say they know someone who takes recreational drugs, while four in ten (42%) say they don't. Older Britons – those aged 60 and above – are much less likely to know a drug user than other age groups. Only 35% do so, compared to 57% of 16–24-year-olds, 66% of 25–39-year-olds and 54% of 40–59-year-olds.

In the 60+ generation, men are likely than women (40% vs 31%) to know someone who takes recreational drugs.

A quarter of Britons (24%) know someone who has a serious problem with drugs. Among Britons who say they themselves have tried drugs, more than a third (36%) know someone who has a drug problem.

One in five (20%) Britons aged 16–24 know someone with a drug problem, which climbs to one in three (32%) of those aged 25–39. Among those in their 40s and 50s, 28% know someone with a drug problem, while this is the case for 17% of those aged 60 or older.

The vast majority of Britons think they can recognise the smell of cannabis

Do you think you can or cannot recognise the smell of cannabis? %

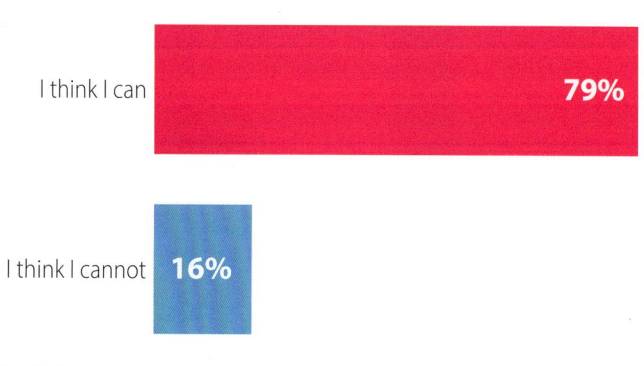

Source: YouGov

Most Britons of all ages have not felt pressured by their peers to take drugs, but younger Brits have experienced it more than older ones

Have you ever felt peer pressure to take recreational drugs? %

- I have felt peer pressured and did end up taking drugs
- I have felt peer pressured but did not end up taking drugs
- I have not felt peer pressured to take recreational drugs

Age	Felt & took	Felt but didn't take	Not felt
16-24	7%	15%	71%
25-39	12%	16%	70%
40-59	7%	11%	80%
60+	2%	6%	92%

Source: YouGov

Most younger Britons know someone who takes recreational drugs, but the majority of over-60s don't

Do you know anyone who takes recreational drugs? %

- I do
- I don't

	All adults	16-24	25-39	40-59	60+
I do	51%	57%	66%	54%	35%
I don't	42%	33%	29%	41%	58%

Source: YouGov

A quarter of Britons say they know someone who has had a serious drug problem

Do you know anyone who has had a serious problem with recreational drugs? %

- I do
- I don't

	All adults	16-24	25-39	40-59	60+
I do	24%	20%	32%	28%	17%
I don't	69%	67%	62%	66%	79%

Source: YouGov

Bearing in mind that cannabis is the most commonly used drug, the YouGov Big Survey on Drugs investigated how familiar Britons are with the smell of the drug. We found that eight out of ten Britons (79%) say they can recognise the smell of cannabis, compared to one in six (16%), who say they cannot.

24 January 2022

The above information is reprinted with kind permission from YouGov.
© 2024 YouGov PLC

www.YouGov.co.uk

Generation X hardest hit as drug deaths rise yet again in England and Wales

An article from The Conversation.

By Ian Hamilton, Honorary Fellow, Department of Health Sciences, University of York and Harry Sumnall, Professor in Substance Use, Liverpool John Moores University

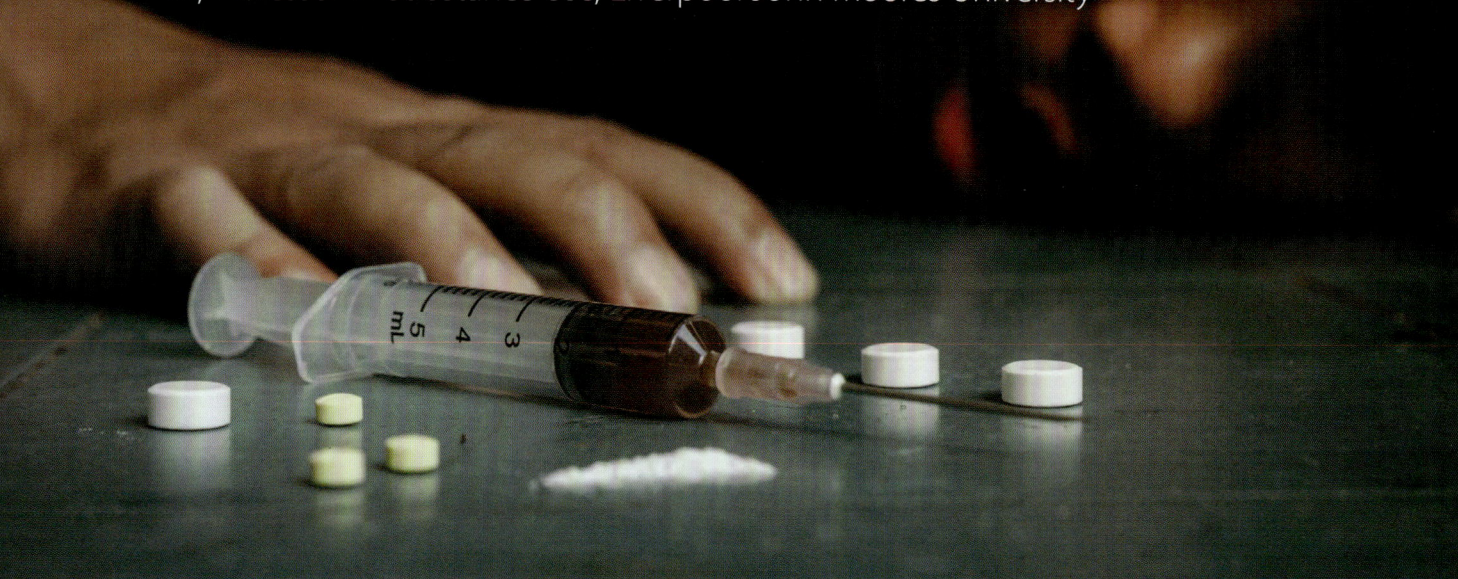

It's another tragic record. A new report has confirmed yet another rise in drug related deaths in England and Wales. The Office for National Statistics (ONS) reports that 4,907 'drug poisoning' deaths were recorded in 2022 (84.4 deaths per 1,000,000 of the population), the highest on record.

While there was a slight fall in deaths in men (from 3,275 in 2021 to 3,240 in 2022), this was masked by a corresponding increase in women (from 1,584 in 2021 to 1,667 in 2022). This reflects a longer term trend of females catching up with male mortality. Drug-related suicides, a topic that doesn't usually receive much attention in discussions about drug-related harms, were also higher in women than men.

Most deaths involved multiple substances, however opiates were detected in just under half of all deaths (2,261 cases).

Of concern are cocaine deaths (857 cases), which have now increased for 11 consecutive years. It's not possible to determine whether these related to use of powder or crack cocaine. But we know there's been an increase in the use of cocaine as well as a boost in the global production, supply, purity, affordability and availability of the drug, despite frequent large seizures by law enforcement agencies.

Cocaine has become more potent and more affordable in recent years. Both factors increase the risk of harm including fatal overdose. We've also lagged behind developing support for people who use cocaine compared to those who use opioids.

Surprisingly, despite its popularity in recreational settings, ketamine is not included in the data – and it is unclear why. Other research suggests there are around 30 deaths each year in England, which is lower than the number of ecstasy deaths (50 in 2022), despite being used by more people.

As for fentanyl, there were tens of thousands of deaths in the US each year. However, in England and Wales these have remained low (57) and stable.

That's reassuring, but it's important not to be complacent. There has been recent concern about the emergence of other types of even more potent opioids, with many experts predicting that these drugs will become more prevalent if opium production in Afghanistan continues to decline – leading to fears of even greater increases in drug deaths.

There were also sharp geographical differences in death rates, with those in more deprived areas in the north east and north west of England much higher than other areas. While there were higher rates of opioid and crack use in these regions, this also reflects wider health and social inequalities.

Age as a risk factor

The highest rate of deaths occurred in the 40- to 49-year-old age group, and the average age at death continued to rise. This is mainly the 'Generation X' cohort born in the 1970s, who came of age when there was a rapid rise in the availability of heroin, and when general population rates of drug use were at their highest in the 1990s.

These premature deaths reflect poorer physical and psychological health, such as compromised respiratory and cardiovascular functioning, which increases the risk of dying from drugs. Many of these health problems could be treated if people accessed health services, but unfortunately too few do – adding to the risk of premature death.

The data doesn't reveal everything though. It is also possible that coroners may record a physical health issue as the cause of death, rather than use of drugs. This adds to an underestimation of the number of people dying from drugs.

Synthetic opioids, implicated in local spikes in deaths, aren't fully captured in the latest ONS figures either. This is because there are delays between when a death occurs, when it is officially recorded by the coroner and when it is included in ONS reports. The latest report includes deaths which occurred in 2021 and 2022, and even as far back as 2017.

While rapid response investigatory panels have been set up in some local areas, these continuing delays hinder rapid assessment of threats to public health.

It may seem paradoxical that overall drug use is declining while drug-related deaths are rising. But this can be explained by the time taken to develop dependent use of drugs and the accompanying problems and risk to health.

Reversing fatalities

The government commissioned Dame Carol Black to advise on how the record number of drug related deaths could be reversed. Her report, published in 2020 and 2021, provided several suggestions including increasing investment in drug treatment which the government has accepted.

While provision of evidence-based drug treatment reduces the risk of death, increased investment will take time to have an impact. It comes after a decade of austerity, which severely affected provision of drug services. Currently, only about half of people who might benefit from formal support are accessing treatment services.

There is no single intervention that will reduce death rates, and the complex profile of the illicit drug market and the cocktail of drugs implicated in deaths means that a whole systems response is required. Most importantly, recent uplifts in funding of treatment services need to be maintained. This will be challenging given the economic pressure on public services.

The priority should be an increase in the community provision of naloxone, the opioid overdose reversal drug. This can already be distributed through drug services, and an increasing number of police officers are also carrying it. Supervised drug consumption facilities, such as the one due to be trialled in Glasgow in 2024 may reduce risks in some more vulnerable groups, including those who are experiencing street homelessness.

City-based drug checking services and local early warning systems can also help to identify the local emergence of harmful substances. The government is also funding pilot projects that may provide technological and data driven innovations.

There remains a worrying lack of innovation in the response to non-opioid drugs such as benzodiazepines (544 deaths this year). Considering the high proportion of deaths attributed to long-term health conditions, it is essential that we continue to break down barriers to accessing timely healthcare in all its forms, including stigma and poor quality care.

20 December 2023

Key Facts

- In 2022 there were 4,907 deaths caused by 'drug poisoning'.
- Deaths from cocaine have increased for 11 consecutive years.
- The highest rate of deaths occurred in the 40- to 49-year-old age group.
- Although drug use is declining, drug-related deaths are rising.

THE CONVERSATION

The above information is reprinted with kind permission from The Conversation.
© 2010-2024, The Conversation Trust (UK) Limited

www.theconversation.com

Prescription drug addiction

When we think about drug addiction, we usually assume that the drugs involved are illegal substances. However, more and more people in the UK and around the world are developing a prescription drug addiction. You may be concerned that you or a loved one may be currently struggling with prescription medication addiction.

Please remember that there is no shame in asking for help.

Benzo addiction

Benzodiazepines are usually provided as medication for a range of conditions such as insomnia, seizures, and anxiety, but can be abused due to the addictive feeling of GABA production. Therefore, being able to identify an addiction is crucial.

Opiate addiction

Opioids are prescribed for pain relief, but abuse can cause an overproduction of pleasure-enhancing dopamine. It is imperative to understand the signs and symptoms of a potential opiate addiction and act quickly to address it.

Sleeping pills addiction

When prescribed for those with sleep disorders, sleeping pills can be beneficial but, if abused, have the potential to be highly addictive.

How prescription drug addiction develops

Prescription drugs such as legal opiates and benzodiazepines can be abused due to their highly addictive qualities. These prescription drugs affect the gamma-aminobutyric acid (GABA) in our brain, a neurotransmitter that produces feelings of calmness.

Whilst benzodiazepines produce GABA, opiates inhibit GABA and replace it with another neurotransmitter: dopamine. Both of these neurotransmitters are pleasure-enhancing. Taking more than your prescribed dosage can facilitate dependency, as your body and mind begin to crave these drugs to receive GABA and dopamine. This is what causes prescription drug abuse, which in turn can result in addiction.

Sadly, recent data has revealed that the estimated proportion of opiate users who are not in rehab or active treatment rose by 5.9% from 2014-2015 to 2019-2020. Likewise, 'more than a quarter of a million people in England' were thought to be taking benzodiazepines and Z-drugs (insomnia medication) 'far beyond the recommended time scales' in 2017.

As prescription medication addiction continues to rise, it is more important than ever to reach out for help if you are worried about a friend, family member, or your own abuse of these substances.

Symptoms of prescription drug abuse

Different types of prescription drug abuse, such as co-codamol addiction, paracetamol addiction, or Ritalin abuse, can produce different symptoms to opiate abuse or benzodiazepine abuse. Here are some of the most common symptoms of prescription medication abuse.

Physical symptoms of prescription drug abuse

- Headaches
- Nausea
- Sweating or high temperature
- Insomnia
- Appetite changes
- Heart palpitations
- Slow breathing
- Digestive problems
- Slurred speech
- Catatonia (immobility)

Psychological symptoms of prescription drug abuse

- Extreme cravings
- Agitation
- Memory problems
- Difficulty concentrating

- Dizziness
- Depression
- Chronic low mood
- Anxiety
- Paranoia
- Confusion

Warning signs of prescription drug addiction

As the symptoms of prescription drug addiction can be physical and psychological, it is not always the easiest mental health disorder to detect. Nonetheless, there are tell-tale signs that you or someone you know may be suffering from prescription medication addiction:

Signs that you have a prescription drug addiction

- Your prescription medication has taken priority above your work or personal life.
- You experience strong cravings for your prescription.
- You feel as if you are physically unable to stop taking your prescription.
- You've visited several doctors to try to get extra prescriptions or placed extra online orders.
- You regularly increase your prescription dosages to achieve feelings of euphoria or calmness.
- You have forged or stolen prescriptions.

Signs a loved one has a prescription drug addiction

- You have noticed that they make very frequent trips to the doctors.
- They present sudden and strong mood swings.
- You have noticed that they are often 'losing' their prescription and requesting new orders on an increasingly frequent basis.
- They are neglecting their responsibilities, such as their career, education, family, and relationships.
- You have noticed that they have become socially withdrawn and secretive.
- They sometimes seem distant and emotionally blunt.

Five things to know about prescription drug addiction

We appreciate that the subject of prescription drug addiction can be upsetting or overwhelming, especially if you believe that you or a loved one may be experiencing this difficult mental health disorder. So, we have provided a short list of the five most important things to know about prescription medication abuse and its risk factors.

1. Prescription drug addiction can be just as dangerous as illicit drug addiction

Anything from paracetamol abuse to opiate abuse can have serious long-term consequences on your mental and physical health. If you abuse prescription medication over an extended period of time, you could experience health complications such as cognitive issues, organ damage, heart problems, respiratory issues, and in the worst case, death.

2. Not all prescription drugs are dangerous

We want to be very clear that you should not suddenly stop taking your medication just because other people have developed addictions to your medication. As long as you take the correct dosages of your prescription at the correct times, you are far less likely to develop prescription drug addiction. Remember that there are lots of contributing factors to prescription drug addiction: genetic, personal history, and social environment. If you are concerned about your dosage or any changes to your prescription, always consult with your doctor to figure out the best course of action.

3. It can be easier for people to hide or lie about prescription drug addiction

Prescription drugs are different to illicit drugs in that they are legal and more accessible. It is easier for prescription medication abuse to hide in plain sight compared to illicit drug abuse.

Therefore, people who are suffering from prescription drug addiction may try to dismiss your concerns about their abuse. For example, they may explain away any mood swings or missing prescriptions as normal behaviour. However, if you see a troubling pattern in their behaviour, you can always offer your support in finding treatment.

4. Some people may struggle to understand prescription drug addiction

Unfortunately, inherited social stereotypes about drug addiction can make it difficult for some people to understand prescription drug addiction. Like alcohol, some may not perceive these substances as overtly dangerous due to their legal status, which can, regrettably, enable a loved one's addiction.

5. You can overcome prescription drug addiction

We are happy to report that there are many avenues of help available for prescription drug abuse in the UK by seeking inpatient or outpatient treatment.

At this stage, you may be wondering how you can find help for prescription drug abuse. If you would like to pursue outpatient support, you can attend a local Narcotics Anonymous support group, which is a fellowship that follows the 12-step programme. Alternatively, you can receive prescription drug addiction treatment at an inpatient UK Addiction Treatment Centres (UKAT) rehab centre which incorporates detox, therapy and one year's free aftercare.

5 December 2023

The above information is reprinted with kind permission from UKAT.
© 2024 UK Addiction Treatment Centres

www.ukat.co.uk

Matthew Perry: the tragedy of extreme addiction is that the body may never recover

The comic star appeared to have achieved sobriety-induced optimism – but drink and drug abuse takes its toll on the body, even in recovery.

By Charlotte Lytton

It was the 'addiction memoir' that laid things bare. Last year, when Matthew Perry released *Friends, Lovers and the Big Terrible Thing*, it detailed his 27-year grapple with drink and drugs in unstinting detail: how he ended up on life support with a 'two% chance to live' after opioid abuse burst his colon, requiring five months of recovery in hospital and nine using a colostomy bag.

That, on another occasion, mixing those opioids with a sedative stopped his heart beating 'for a full five minutes'; there too were the 14 operations he had on his stomach, the period of erectile dysfunction, and the day where, after biting into a slice of toast, all of his top teeth fell out (Perry carried them to his dentist in his jeans pocket).

By 49, more than half of his life – and $9 million – had been spent in treatment facilities. That Big Terrible Thing was in fact not one entity, but many, often resulting in his drinking 14 triple shots of vodka or taking 55 prescription painkillers a day.

The youthful bounce of Perry's early days as Chandler Bing, the sarcastic *Friends* stalwart who would become an international star, soon began shifting in ways that could not have been age alone. 'When I'm carrying weight, it's alcohol; when I'm skinny, it's pills. When I have a goatee, it's lots of pills,' he explained in his book of his changing appearance on the show.

It was so striking that the most commonly asked question his co-star Lisa Kudrow would receive about *Friends*, she wrote in the memoir's foreword, was 'how's Matthew Perry doing?'

The answer, when it was released last November, appeared to be well. Terrified by his latest brush with death and the prospect of needing a permanent colostomy bag, Perry was 18 months sober and, for the first time, ready to admit the extremes his addictions had taken him to. 'I feel better because it's out,' he said. 'It's on a piece of paper' – one that, incredibly rarely for celebrity memoirs, he had written every word of himself.

'I wanted to share when I was safe from going into the dark side again,' he said in another interview. 'I had to wait until I was pretty safely sober – and away from the active disease of alcoholism and addiction' to come clean. One reviewer called *Friends, Lovers and the Big Terrible Thing* 'a scream of authentic pain.'

While deeply exposing, writing the book had made Perry 'stronger in every way'. Yet the ostensibly stable world he had been navigating would provide the backdrop to his death on Saturday aged just 54, when he was found drowned in his jacuzzi, of a suspected cardiac arrest.

Perry had reportedly played two hours of pickleball that morning – a sport he had become so fond of as to build a court at his Los Angeles home – before his assistant returned to find him unresponsive.

No illegal drugs were found (though a police 'mole' did report finding prescription drugs for chronic obstructive pulmonary disease and antidepressants at his home), and no foul play is suspected. The results of an initial post-mortem are inconclusive, according to US media reports, with an official conclusion not expected for several weeks. His last photo (six days before his death) posted to Instagram, of himself in the water, headphones on, under the dark of the night sky, has taken on a haunting air.

Perry was cast in *Friends* in 1994 at the age of 24, the wry foil to his co-stars' more cookie-cutter characters. The show would transform their lives, with each of its ten series earning tens of millions of viewers; 52 million people tuned into the 2004 finale, the show's success by that stage so fundamental to the zeitgeist as to earn its cast $1 million apiece per episode. Close to two decades since it concluded, Bing is routinely voted viewers' favourite character.

As the show's success soared, behind the scenes, Perry was struggling. He was first given prescription painkillers in 1997, following a jet ski accident on the set of *Fools Rush In* with Salma Hayek; within 18 months, he was taking 55 Vicodin a day – a cocktail so potent that he later admitted he couldn't remember shooting three seasons of *Friends*. The more he took, the more he needed to take in order to replicate the buzz, taking to attending open-house viewings on Sundays and raiding owners' medicine cabinets, in order to remain topped up.

'It's exhausting but you have to do it or you get very, very sick,' he said of the prospect of withdrawal. 'I wasn't doing it to feel high or to feel good. I certainly wasn't a partier; I just wanted to sit on my couch, take five Vicodin, and watch a movie. That was heaven for me.'

On set, things were becoming harder to conceal. While Perry said he was never high during filming, the effects of what he was doing the rest of the time made themselves known: he fell asleep during one scene, nudged awake by co-star Matt LeBlanc as he was due to say his line; his onscreen wedding to Monica (Courteney Cox) in 2001 wrapped with him being driven back to a treatment centre. 'At the height of my highest point in *Friends*, the highest point in my career, the iconic moment on the iconic show – [I was] in a pickup truck helmed by a sober technician.'

There was the time Jennifer Aniston came to his trailer and told him that his co-stars could smell the alcohol he was consuming in vast quantities; on another occasion, the cast confronted him in his dressing room. All had remained close in the 19 years since wrapping, with Kudrow last year describing Perry's battle with 'a hideous disease, and he has a tough version of it.'

The tragedy of his death after fighting so long to get clean highlights the toll drink and drug abuse can take on the body, even once abstinent. Common by-products of excess consumption include liver disease such as hepatitis or cirrhosis, kidney damage, collapsed veins and bacterial infections, bowel disease, emphysema, and raised risk of aneurysms and stroke.

'Drink affects pretty much every organ in the body, but particularly the liver and the heart and the immune system,' explains David Nutt, Professor of Neuropsychopharmacology at Imperial College London and author of *Drugs Without the Hot Air*. 'If you've damaged yourself [from excess drug use], you'll almost certainly reduce your life expectancy, which is why it's always better not to do that in the first place.'

Research published last year showed that 22.35 million adults in the US (equivalent to 9.1%) were living in recovery, but there are limited studies showing how organs readjust once consumption of toxic substances ends, with the prevailing theory being that some – but not all – damage can be reversed.

Researchers from Oregon Health & Science University in 2018 showed that even limited exposure to cocaine could fundamentally alter neuronal circuits in the brain, while a 2021 paper from the journal *Alcohol Research: Current Reviews* found that after excess drinking, 'damaged organs may regain partial function or even heal completely, depending on the extent of organ damage and whether there is relapse.'

Its authors noted too that alcohol-induced dilated cardiomyopathy – where part of the heart muscle becomes stretched, making it unable to pump blood as it should – was prevalent in those who drank to excess, and was 'accompanied by a high incidence of cardiac morbidity and mortality.'

While ceasing substance abuse will inevitably improve any conditions it has caused, 'the likelihood is you'll probably get a bit better, but I don't think you'll fully recover,' says Nutt. A toxicology report concluded the same condition had afflicted George Michael, a heavy drink and drug user until his death in 2016, aged 53.

Perry knew well that curbing his use of drink and drugs was not the end of the road, with recovery being, as it is for all addicts, 'a day-to-day process of getting better.' He cared deeply about helping others in its grip – certain that 'if a selfish lazy f— like myself can change, then anyone can' – at one stage setting up a sober rehab facility, the Perry House, at his former Malibu home.

Dedicating his book to 'all of the sufferers out there,' he began finding purpose in speaking out about what he had endured. 'Sometimes I think I went through the addiction, alcoholism and fame all to be doing what I'm doing right now, which is helping people.'

Sober, he wanted more for himself, too. At the time of his book's release (which sold double the number of copies as Bono's memoir), he spoke of how addiction had derailed his personal relationships. Long-term happiness had proved elusive, he said, 'because I won't allow myself to have it. I always think something's going to go wrong.'

Following relationships with actresses including Julia Roberts, Lizzy Caplan and Neve Campbell, he proposed to literary agent Molly Hurwitz in 2020 – while 'high as a kite' on 1,800mg of painkiller hydrocodone. They split soon afterwards; another missed opportunity to start the family he had craved.

'Had I done so, I would not now be sitting in a huge house overlooking the ocean, with no one to share it with save a nurse, a sober companion, and a gardener twice a week,' he wrote.

But optimism – perhaps induced by that sobriety – had by last year begun to creep in. 'I think I'd be a great father,' he said in an interview around the time of his book's release, mulling an altogether different role. 'I'm feeling more confident and I'm not afraid of love anymore.'

30 October 2023

The above information is reprinted with kind permission from *The Telegraph*.
© Telegraph Media Group Limited 2023

www.telegraph.co.uk

Taking laughing gas 600 times a week left me in a wheelchair

A woman left paralysed and in a wheelchair after taking 600 canisters of laughing gas a week has welcomed it being made illegal.

By Jasper King

Kerry-Anne Donaldson, 26, from Newham, London, became addicted to the high of nitrous oxide (NOS) at parties at the age of 18.

By the age of 21 her legs and feet went numb and she ended up in a wheelchair.

The numbness has now spread to her hands and after pushing herself to walk with crutches, she struggles like never before.

The Class C drug will be made illegal from 8 November as part of a government crackdown on antisocial behaviour.

Speaking after yesterday's announcement Kerry-Anne said: 'I don't think the law will get it off the streets. If someone wants it, there will always be a way to buy it,

'Kids have always found a way to get illegal drugs, so I'm not sure it will actually stop them, but it should at least push up the prices and prevent overuse.'

She added: 'As soon as I woke up I would get straight on the balloons,

'I kept chasing the original high I felt, but because my head was already rushing, I couldn't find it,

'I now can't move my legs and have to take a lot of pain medication while living out of a wheelchair,

'When taking the balloons I would barely eat so I am now anaemic and the shortness of breath has affected my asthma,

'My dad is primary carer, and I'm so lucky to have so much support around me, from him, my mum, and my sisters. I don't know what I would do without them.'

It was when Kerry-Anne was 21 that she first noticed the impact it was having on her body and she went to the doctor.

What is nitrous oxide?

Nitrous oxide is a gas legally used in medicine and catering.

It is often sold in smaller silver canisters for catering and events and this is usually how users get hold of it.

The most common way to do NOS as a drug is to transfer the gas into a balloon and inhale the balloon.

Some people inhale the NOS straight from the canister but this is extremely dangerous.

The desired effect is to feel giggly, relaxed, euphoric, and distort reality. It can also make people feel anxious, paranoid, and dizzy. The effects only last for about two minutes.

The gas works by temporarily preventing oxygen from reaching the blood.

She said: 'He [the doctor] said the reason I'm in pain and unable to walk is because of the damage it causes,

'It blocks oxygen from going around your body and to your brain and destroys your vitamin B12 levels.'

When Kerry-Anne was put in a wheelchair and started to recover she began inhaling the gas again from 'morning to night'.

She then developed a vitamin B12 deficiency after her legs went numb which caused her to stop taking the substance again.

She was also bedbound for months, relying on assistance from family and friends for the simplest tasks like showering and getting dressed.

'About a month ago I started to struggle using my hands, having to use both to drink from a glass,' she said.

'The doctor said my folic acid and iron is low, but they haven't been very helpful over the past few years other than prescribing pain medicine and they've recently referred me to the pain clinic.'

She is pleased the new laws will hopefully get the previously accessible drug off the streets as she feels strongly about saving other teenagers from the same fate.

'I started my TikTok @_theydontloveyou and posted videos about my story, and some went viral,' she said.

'I feel like maybe this was my calling – to help others, and it's really improved my mental health, which was never great even before the balloons.'

19 October 2023

The above information is reprinted with kind permission from *Metro*.
© 2024 Associated Newspapers Ltd

www.metro.co.uk

Chapter 2

Drugs and the Law

Drugs and the law

Legal drugs

Some drugs are legal, like caffeine, nicotine, and alcohol. Also, prescribed and over-the-counter medications are legal if used correctly. However, their use may be restricted based on age, location of use, and rules around where they're sold. For example, in the UK it is illegal to buy cigarettes if you are under 18. If you are under 16 the police have the right to confiscate any cigarettes you may have on you.

There are also restrictions on driving when under the influence of alcohol or certain prescribed medications.

Legal drugs are also regulated and controlled so that the active ingredients, and alcohol or nicotine content, are consistent across the products.

Understanding drug classification

To comprehend the legal status of various drugs, it's crucial to understand the classification system in the UK. The Misuse of Drugs Act 1971 is the law that classifies drugs based on their potential harm and the penalties associated with their possession, supply, and production.

Class A drugs

Class A drugs are considered to have the highest potential for harm and carry the most severe legal consequences. Examples of Class A drugs include heroin, cocaine, ecstasy, LSD, and magic mushrooms (when they contain the chemical psilocin). Possessing or supplying these substances can result in lengthy prison sentences and hefty fines.

Class B drugs

Class B drugs, such as cannabis, amphetamines, and ketamine, are considered to have a lower potential for harm than Class A drugs. However, they are still illegal and can lead to serious legal repercussions. Possession can result in up to five years in prison, while supply or production can lead to up to 14 years' imprisonment.

Class C drugs

Class C drugs, like anabolic steroids, benzodiazepines, and certain tranquillisers, are considered to have the lowest potential harm among illegal drugs. Possessing a Class C drug can result in up to two years' imprisonment and an unlimited fine. Supplying or producing Class C drugs may lead to a prison sentence of up to 14 years.

Legal highs and temporary bans

Some substances, commonly referred to as 'legal highs' or new psychoactive substances (NPS), fall outside the traditional drug classification system. So-called 'legal highs' are anything but. The Psychoactive Substances Act 2016 gave authorities the power to ban the production and supply of these substances, which mimic the effects of illegal drugs without being specifically controlled. Possessing and supplying 'legal highs' can result in consequences similar to those associated with Class A, B, and C drugs.

The consequences of drug offences

It's important to understand the potential consequences of drug offences to make informed decisions and avoid unnecessary risks. If caught in possession of drugs, even in small quantities, you may be arrested and taken to a police station for questioning. The police have the authority to search individuals and their property if they suspect drug possession.

Upon arrest, the police can release you on bail or keep you in custody, depending on the circumstances. If the case goes to court and you are found guilty of drug offences, the potential penalties can be severe. These include substantial fines, a criminal record, and even imprisonment, depending on the drug involved and the scale of the offence.

Furthermore, a drug conviction can have long-term consequences, affecting one's career prospects, travel opportunities, and personal relationships. It's crucial to weigh the potential risks against any perceived benefits when it comes to drug use.

Seeking support and advice

If you or someone you know is struggling with drug misuse, it's important to seek support. Various organisations, such as Talk to Frank and local drug advisory services, offer confidential help and guidance for those dealing with drug-related issues. Education, awareness, and open conversations can make a significant difference in tackling drug misuse.

Understanding the laws surrounding drugs is an essential step in making informed choices that can positively impact our lives. By familiarising ourselves with drug classifications and the potential consequences of drug offences, we empower ourselves to navigate this complex topic responsibly. Remember, knowledge is key, and staying informed helps us maintain our well-being and make informed decisions. Don't hesitate to reach out for support when needed, and always prioritise your health and safety above all else.

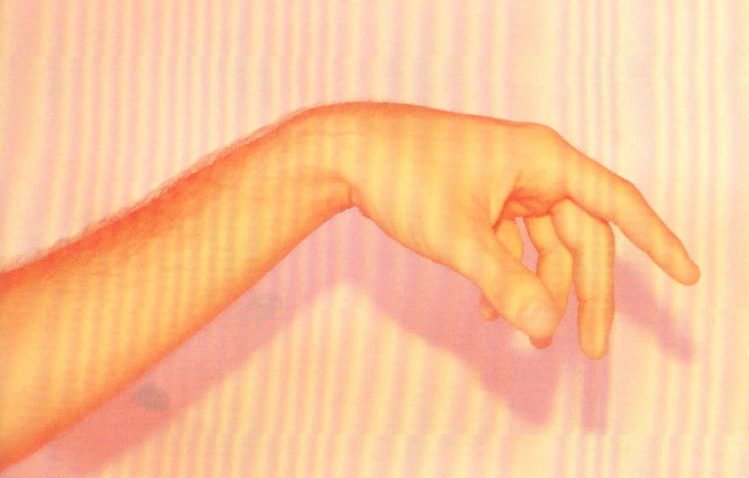

Drugs penalties

You can get a fine or prison sentence if you:

- Take drugs
- Carry drugs
- Make drugs
- Sell, deal or share drugs (also called 'supplying' them)

The penalties depend on the type or 'class' of drug or substance, the amount you have, and whether you're also dealing or producing it.

Class A

Class A drugs include:

- Cocaine
- Crack cocaine
- Ecstasy (MDMA)
- Heroin
- LSD
- Magic mushrooms
- Methadone
- Methamphetamine (crystal meth).

Class B

Class B drugs include:

- Amphetamines
- Barbiturates
- Cannabis
- Codeine
- Gamma hydroxybutyrate (GHB)
- Gamma-butyrolactone (GBL)
- Ketamine
- Methylphenidate (Ritalin)
- Synthetic cannabinoids
- Synthetic cathinones (for example mephedrone, methoxetamine).

Class C

Class C drugs include:

- Anabolic steroids
- Benzodiazepines (diazepam)
- Khat
- Nitrous oxide (laughing gas)
- Piperazines (BZP).

Temporary class drugs

The government can ban new drugs for one year under a 'temporary banning order' while they decide how the drugs should be classified.

Penalties for drug possession, supply, and production

The maximum penalties for drug possession, supply (selling, dealing, or sharing), and production depend on the drug class.

Psychoactive substances penalties

Psychoactive substances are things that cause:

- Hallucinations
- Drowsiness
- Changes in alertness
- Changes in perception of time and space
- Changes in mood or empathy with others.

Penalties for drug possession, supply and production

The maximum penalties for drug possession, supply (selling, dealing or sharing) and production depend on the drug class.

	Maximum penalty for possession	Maximum penalty for supply and production
Class A	Up to 7 years in prison, an unlimited fine or both	Up to life in prison, an unlimited fine or both
Class B	Up to 5 years in prison, an unlimited fine or both	Up to 14 years in prison, an unlimited fine or both
Class C	Up to 2 years in prison, an unlimited fine or both (except anabolic steroids - it's not an offence to possess them for personal use)	Up to 14 years in prison, an unlimited fine or both
Temporary class drugs	None, but police can take away a suspected temporary class drug	Up to 14 years in prison, an unlimited fine or both

Source: Gov.UK

Food, alcohol, nicotine, caffeine, medicine, and illegal drugs do not count as psychoactive substances.

Possession penalty

There is no penalty for carrying psychoactive substances, unless you're in prison.

Supply and production penalty

You can get up to seven years in prison, an unlimited fine, or both if you:

- Carry a psychoactive substance and you intend to supply it
- Make a psychoactive substance
- Sell, deal, or share a psychoactive substance (also called supplying them).

Possessing drugs

You may be charged with possessing an illegal substance if you're caught with drugs, whether they're yours or not.

If you're under 18, the police are allowed to tell your parent, guardian, or carer that you've been caught with drugs.

Your penalty will depend on:

- The class and quantity of drug
- Where you and the drugs were found
- Your personal history (previous crimes, including any previous drug offences)
- Other aggravating or mitigating factors.

Cannabis and khat

Police can issue a warning or an on-the-spot fine of up to £90 if you're found with cannabis or khat. You may be able to pay your penalty without getting a formal warning or caution.

If you're repeatedly found with cannabis or khat, your penalty may vary from treatment to their maximum penalty for possession.

Dealing or supplying drugs

The penalty is likely to be more severe if you are found to be supplying drugs (dealing, selling, or sharing).

The police will probably charge you if they suspect you of supplying drugs. The amount of drugs found and whether you have a criminal record will affect your penalty.

The above information is reprinted with kind permission from GOV.UK
© Crown Copyright 2024
This information is licensed under the Open Government Licence v3.0
To view this licence, visit http://www.nationalarchives.gov.uk/doc/open-government-licence/

www.gov.uk

Is it time to consider decriminalising drugs in the UK?

With the recent sharp rise in drug-related deaths in the UK, the government should consider radical policy action to halt a public health crisis. One option would be to draw on lessons from abroad and decriminalise recreational narcotics.

By Jake Taibel, University of Bristol

Years of futile efforts to eradicate the use of drugs in the UK has only exacerbated vicious circles of crime and poverty. Change is necessary.

Decriminalisation would focus on harm reduction, rehabilitation, and reframing how society views drug users. Healthcare services and the criminal justice system would endure less stress, freeing up money that the government can redirect into treatment and community services. Further, rehabilitation and reintegration of previous drug users back into the workforce would have a positive effect on the individuals in question, their employers, and the government.

Among the UK public, views on drug addicts are progressive. A sample from YouGov finds that 49% of people feel that those 'who have addictions to illegal substances should be treated as those who are mentally ill would be treated.' Just 19% are against this view. So, UK policymakers should consider what the electorate want, and investigate a more liberal approach.

As the cost-of-living crisis continues, the Resolution Foundation expects 1.3 million people to fall into absolute poverty. Evidence suggests that higher levels of poverty result in higher rates of addiction. This is not because of choice or physical dependence, but more a result of social exclusions such as structural disadvantages and limited opportunities. In 2004, Julian Buchanan (Victoria University of Wellington) said that what is needed is 'social integration not social reintegration, they need 'habilitation' not rehabilitation'.

Drug misuse is costing society an enormous £19.3 billion a year, 86% of which is attributable to the health and crime-related costs of the heroin and crack cocaine markets. These findings by Dame Carol Black extend to explain that only 3% is spent on treatment and prevention, despite Public Health England reporting that every pound spent on drug treatment saves £2.50 in costs to society. If the government were to invest in social policies, there would be better social outcomes for all, including communities feeling safer.

Portugal became the first country to decriminalise drug use in 2001, attempting to turn around an opioid epidemic. A 2014 report found that Portugal's per capita social cost of drug misuse decreased by 18%.

This success is thanks to investment in prevention and social care schemes. A report in *The Guardian* explains that one support scheme offers a drop-in centre with 'psychologists, doctors, and peer support workers offering clean needles, crack kits... rapid HIV testing, and consultations'. This emphasis on harm reduction enabled Portugal's yearly new HIV rate per million to fall by 95.97% between 2000 and 2015.

Analysis in the *New York Times* finds that Portugal now has the lowest drug-related death rate in Western Europe, with a mortality rate a tenth of the UK's and a fiftieth of the United States.' Portugal's improvements are starkly different to the UK, where drug-related deaths are at a record high, having seen a 75.6% increase from 2012 to 2020. These statistics should alarm the UK government: decriminalising drugs could save thousands of lives.

Researchers at the London School of Economics have found that austerity measures have been a driver of these outcomes, with areas experiencing the biggest cuts to social care and housing services seeing the highest death tolls. This is a serous concern in the context of the current cost-of-living crisis and the lack of support from the government.

It could culminate in greater poverty, crime, and inequality, all of which are in a vicious circle with drug use. If poverty continues to increase, health and policing services will face a further strain.

A concern of those opposed to decriminalising drugs is a potential increase in drug use, as consequences weaken significantly. But Caitlin Hughes and Alex Stevens (Drug Policy Alliance) find little evidence of this in Portugal, where usage has stayed relatively constant while seeing 'a reduction in problematic usage, drug-related harms, and criminal justice overcrowding.'

The Mayor of London, Sadiq Khan, proposed a trial that would decriminalise cannabis in three London boroughs in January 2022, but this is yet to be approved. Despite criminal

justice and public health experts responding positively, the government believes otherwise, with former minister Priti Patel claiming that drugs 'ruin communities, tear apart families, and destroy lives.'

The current government made a ten-year plan to combat drug-related crime in 2021. One proposed policy involved removing passports and driving licences from middle-class 'lifestyle' users of class A drugs. It should be noted that a dozen sites inside the Palace of Westminster tested positive for traces of cocaine in 2021.

UK policymakers have been found to break laws over and over again. Why do we allow them to continue legislating laws that seem to contradict expert evidence? For such a serious issue as drug abuse, which results in thousands of deaths, political standpoints should be left aside and let protecting human life come first.

2 January 2023
This article is from the University of Bristol's Communicating Economics class of 2022-2023.

Key Facts

- Drug misuse is costs society £19.3 billion a year.
- Portugal was the first country to decriminalise drug use in 2021.
- Portugal now has the lowest drug-related death rate in Western Europe.

The above information is reprinted with kind permission from Economics Observatory.
© 2024 Economics Observatory
www.economicsobservatory.com

Has the time come for reform of the UK's drug policy?

By Albert Ward

Unlike in many other countries, the UK's drug policy has seen little development in recent years. Are concerns that liberalisation would not have public support well-founded? Albert Ward finds public support for significant reform is promising but capricious, and easily influenced by how questions are asked.

What is the future for drug reform in the UK? While other countries have already legalised recreational use marijuana or gone further, decriminalising hard drugs like cocaine and heroin, the UK drugs regime has not changed much in the last few decades. Many more countries have implemented minor policies, such as supervised consumption or the medical use of hard drugs.

Much hesitance from policymakers and the media comes from the impression that the public would be opposed to any attempt at liberalisation. How true is this? Evidence from a range of polling sources reveals that people in the UK have subtle preferences for liberalisation of drug laws, which can vary greatly depending on which options are presented to them and how questions are asked.

No blanket support for legalisation

Much of the current debate centres on legalisation. When it comes to marijuana legalisation – the most-used illegal drug in the UK and the most obvious candidate for liberalisation – the public is split. A poll by Redfield and Winton in 2022 found 38% opposed to 35% in favour, with 20% neither supporting nor opposing and 7% stating they 'don't know.'

Question wording and presentation is key, though. Remove that 'neither' option, as a 2019 YouGov poll did, and give people who do not support either side outright the option to 'tend to support/oppose', and 53% support such legalisation, against 31% opposed, with 15% 'don't knows'. Note also, however, that most polls ignore the subtle difference between decriminalisation (removing criminal sanctions, and potentially replacing them with civil penalties, while drugs still remain illegal) and legalisation (removing all penalties for possession and personal use).

When it comes to legalisation of hard drugs, public opposition is far higher and more stable.

A 2022 YouGov survey found 86% in support of keeping such drugs illegal (the survey offered only the choice between legal, illegal but not criminal, and illegal and criminal). Other surveys demonstrate similar levels of support. Similarly, people tend to be far less forgiving of distributors and sellers of drugs: 71% in that same YouGov poll thought that selling soft drugs should be illegal, while 89% believed the same for hard drugs.

A nuanced picture on punitive measures

Still, this general opposition to legalisation does not necessarily translate into support for strict penalties. While large numbers of Britons are supportive of harsh sentences for relatively minor crimes, 61% support handing those caught personally using drugs – technically in danger of long jail time – community service sentences or less. If you ask people directly to choose what punishments should be meted out for personal use possession, the top two results – beating prison by 30% – are education or treatment (54% of people chose) and a fine (49%).

Again, however, question wording muddies the picture. If you ask Brits whether, in general, they think drug laws in the UK are too strict or too lenient, 40% agree with the latter, while only 19% with the former (24% think they are about right). People even think stricter laws would be effective, at least in some areas. A majority – 53% – believe that harsher punishments would deter distribution and sale of illegal drugs, despite all evidence to the contrary.

Part of this confusion may come down to a lack of awareness of what penalties are applied to different drug offences, or to large differences between the penalties people think should apply to soft and hard drugs, which have not been captured by pollsters, at least in recent surveys. It may also be that, while people have a generalised sense that the current drugs regime is failing and should be stricter, when presented with specific options, they soften their stance.

Evidence of a shift away from a criminalising approach?

There is some evidence for this with minor liberalisation measures, where public support is far higher than the inconsistent evidence for legalisation. Clear majorities of people in the UK support overdose prevention centres, drug safety checking services, or the ready availability of anti-overdose drugs. This reflects a general support for a refocusing of drug policy towards health and addiction treatment rather than as a principally criminal issue. It might also be that the middling enthusiasm for decriminalisation or legalisation is a lower bound of the true level of support, which people may be unwilling to divulge to pollsters.

> 'Clear majorities of people in the UK support overdose prevention centres, drug safety checking services, or the ready availability of anti-overdose drugs.'

The survey which found the highest outright support for marijuana legalisation, not counting a 'tend to' option: a 2022 Redfield and Winton poll, which prefaced the question with a short explanation of what such a policy would look like. It found 48% in favour, with 27% opposed (18% expressed neither, and 6% 'don't know'). This suggests that public preferences for at least some aspects of drug policy are malleable, and sensitive to explanation of the issues at hand. Information scarcity may play a role. 58% of people in the UK are not at all or only slightly aware of current drug policy (note that the wording implies alcohol and tobacco are considered drugs in this survey).

The War on Drugs is, in terms of efficacy, a strong candidate for the worst public policy decision of the last fifty years, almost wherever you are in the world. For something which the vast majority of Britons believe is not working – nearly two-thirds think criminalising drugs is an ineffective way of preventing their use – there is clearly desire for reform.

Support for change is capricious, however; it varies greatly depending on what options people are presented with, and how questions are worded. If there is to be policy change, politicians must therefore take great care to consider public opinion. This does not mean that they should reject radical solutions. Legalisation and decriminalisation can be effective at reducing drug harm, if not use; we should thus not discount them. Such policies can be hard to sell to voters, though. If they are to be considered in the UK, they should be part of a programme of reform, which includes efforts to reduce drug-related crime and lessen addiction. Their effect and their implementation must be explained, accompanied by a real effort to inform people. Most importantly perhaps, they must appear part of a logical progression of policies, and not seem like they are an unwarranted change forced upon people.

14 March 2023

This blogpost gives the views of the author(s), and not the position of LSE British Politics and Policy, nor of the London School of Economics and Political Science.

Key Facts
- A 2022 YouGov survey found 86% in support of keeping hard drugs illegal.

Research

Create a questionnaire to find out people's opinions on whether or not drugs should be legalised in the UK.

Are people generally for or against legalisation?

Are people more likely to support legalisation of 'soft' drugs compared to 'hard' drugs?

Are there any differences in opinions in the ages or genders?

The above information is reprinted with kind permission from LSE.
© LSE 2024

www.blogs.lse.ac.uk

Should possessing or selling drugs be legal?

By Milan Dinic

Four in ten Britons (40%) think that UK drug laws are too soft, while one in five (19%) think they are too strict, and a quarter (24%) think they are about right.

Men are more likely than women to think that UK laws on drugs are too strict (22% vs 15%). Younger Britons are also likely to see the drug laws as being too strict: 30% among those aged 18–24, compared to 21% of 25–39 year olds, and 12–17% among those aged 40 and older.

For the purposes of this study, we refer to soft drugs (such as cannabis or speed) and hard drugs (such as cocaine or heroin).

Three in ten Britons (30%) think that the possession of soft drugs such as cannabis should be legal providing it is for personal use only. A third (33%) think possessing soft drugs for personal use should be illegal but treated as a minor offence, while a quarter (25%) say it should be a criminal offence.

A political breakdown of the results shows that twice as many Labour voters as Conservatives (41% vs 19%) back legalising the possession of soft drugs.

When asked whether selling soft drugs should be legal, one in five Britons (19%) support this. Again, there is a strong political divide here: 10% of Conservative voters support the idea, compared to nearly a quarter (23%) of those who voted Labour.

One in four (24%) think the sale of soft drugs should be illegal but not criminalised, while nearly half of Britons (47%) think this should be a criminal offence.

Younger Britons are more likely than older ones to say drug laws in the UK are too strict, while older Brits say they're too lenient

Generally speaking, do you think drug laws in the UK are too strict, too lenient, or about right? %

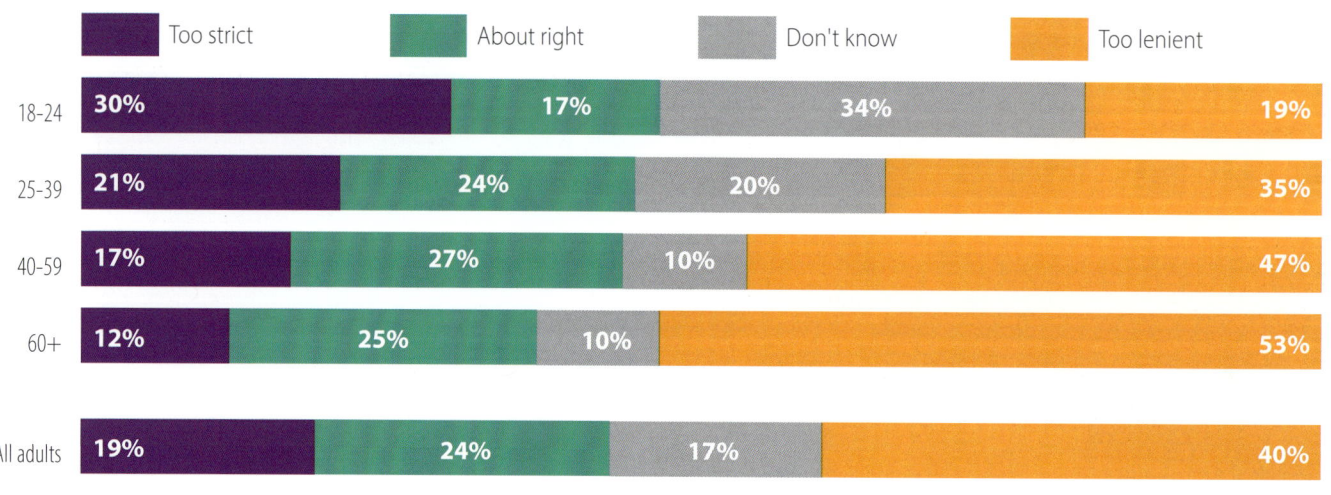

Source: YouGov

Three in ten Britons think possession of soft drugs, like cannabis and speed, should be legal, but almost half still believe selling them should be a criminal offence

Do you think [the possession with the intention of personal use]/[selling] soft drugs (such as cannabis or speed) should be legal or illegal? %

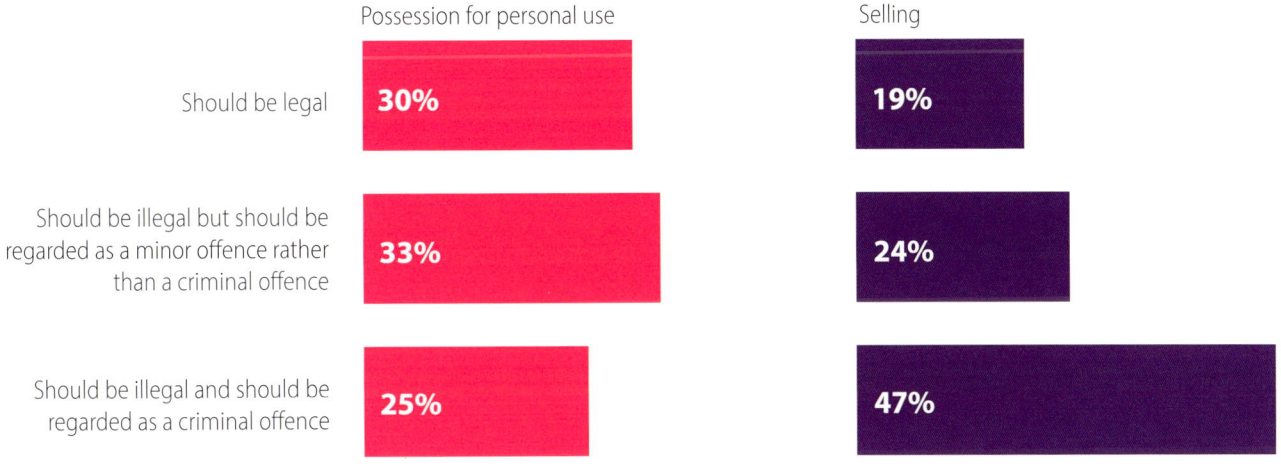

Source: YouGov

The vast majority of Britons think both possession and selling of hard drugs, like heroin and crack cocaine, should be a criminal offence

Do you think [the possession with the intention of personal use]/[selling] hard drugs (such as heroin or crack cocaine) should be legal or illegal? %

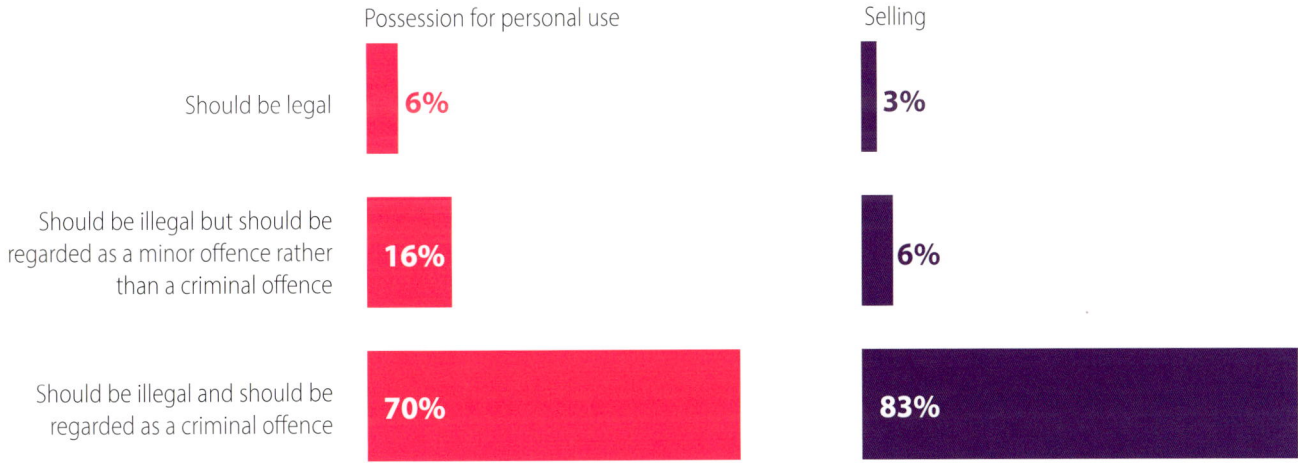

Source: YouGov

Two-thirds of Britons (64%) who say they take hard/soft drugs think that the sale of soft drugs should be legalised, while just 7% of them say it should be a criminal offence.

6% of Britons think that possessing hard drugs – such as heroin or cocaine – for personal use should be legal.

Seven in ten Britons (70%) think that the possession of hard drugs should be a criminal offence, with significantly more Conservatives (85%) than Labour voters (60%) backing this.

One in six (16%) say possessing hard drugs should be considered a minor offence. Again, this view is shared more by Labour (24%) than Conservative (7%) voters.

A quarter of Britons who currently use hard/soft drugs (26%) say possessing hard drugs should be legal, half (51%) think it should be a minor offence, while 22% say it should be a criminal offence.

The story is different when it comes to the issue of selling hard drugs: just 3% of Britons support legalising this and 6% say it should be illegal but a minor offence. Eight in ten (83%) think that the sale of hard drugs should be a criminal offence.

Overall, men are more likely than women to be more lenient when it comes to the legality of drug possession and selling. Older Britons – those aged 60 and above – tend to take a somewhat harder line on the issue than younger age groups.

24 January 2022

The above information is reprinted with kind permission from YouGov.
© 2024 YouGov PLC

www.YouGov.co.uk

UK drug policy: how seizing passports will not stop illicit drug use

An article from The Conversation.

By Tammy Ayres Lecturer in Criminology, University of Leicester and Stuart Taylor, The Open University

In an attempt to clamp down on recreational drug use, the British government recently set out a three-tier system for dealing with people caught in possession of illegal substances.

A scale of punishments would be introduced for those caught in possession once, twice or three times. These would begin with a fine and culminate in a variety of deeply punitive options such as tagging offenders, suspending their driving licence and even confiscating their passport.

All this is being promoted as part of a government plan, entitled Swift, Certain, Tough: new consequences for drug possession, which aims to bring overall drug use down to 'a historic 30-year low' by 'delivering a generational shift in demand'.

Other nations, including the US, Jamaica and Thailand are modernising their drug policies and moving away from criminalisation. The UK, meanwhile, seems determined to disregard the evidence that has for decades contradicted the idea that ever-tougher responses are needed.

Research has long shown that punitive measures are not a deterrent. Further, most illegal drug use is recreational, more commonly associated with leisure and pleasure than criminality. Research shows that recreational drug use rarely leads to addiction or requires treatment.

The government seems far from understanding this, as is evident when it calls drugs the 'root of untold harm and misery across our society' in its reform proposals. It is questionable whether this reductionist discourse applies to any drug user – there are, for example, functioning heroin addicts who live normal productive lives – let alone recreational drugs and their users.

Evidence shows criminalising otherwise law-abiding citizens for their drug use does not deter them from doing it. In fact, it merely serves to damage their life chances.

We know that a conviction makes it harder for people (and particularly young people) to find housing, get a job and travel. It also makes them more likely to continue offending. All this should make the government think long and hard about which offences therefore justify serious punishment.

Punitive measures are discriminatory in practice

Drug laws and their punishments are not applied equitably and tend to discriminate along the lines of class, and gender, as we have already seen with cannabis warnings.

Cannabis warnings are issued by the police for those found in possession of a small amount of cannabis and operate as the first stage of a similar three-tiered escalation system implemented to deal with cannabis use.

And when it comes to race, they discriminate too. In London, black people, often from deprived areas, receive cannabis warnings at three times the rate of white people.

Law enforcement measures are being used to deter recreational drug use, while more harmful substances such as alcohol, tobacco and sugar remain legal and socially acceptable. This, despite the research being clear on how such substances cause more harm than many of their illicit counterparts. A truly evidence-based approach to drugs would look very different.

The proposed new 'three-tier' approach may appear to be a reform but the reality is that while the government's proposed punishments for first and second offences may appear to err towards decriminalisation, the punishments for third offences – tagging offenders, suspending their driving licences and confiscating their passports – are extreme.

Ultimately, this remains a law enforcement approach that has already been shown to be ineffective. It will not bring overall drug use down. It will, however, undoubtedly cause untold harm to thousands of people.

Instead of focusing on low-level possession of recreational drugs, we need realistic, effective, evidence-based ways to reduce the harms of drugs, in terms of use and supply. We also need to support those drug users who want support, rather than inflicting punishments that will disproportionately criminalise certain groups of users.

13 October 2022

Debate

Debate the need for consequences for illegal drug possession and use. Half of the class will be for bringing in tougher consequences, the other half against.

THE CONVERSATION

The above information is reprinted with kind permission from The Conversation.
© 2010-2024, The Conversation Trust (UK) Limited

www.theconversation.com

Illegal muscle-building drugs being sold in UK shops, says report

Pharmacists body demand stricter laws against drug use and selling.

By Shweta Sharma

Illegal muscle-building drugs are being reportedly sold in shops as well as on online platforms in the UK, according to a report.

Body-building supplements with substances known as selective androgen receptor modulators (SARMs) are not authorised for sale in the UK.

An investigation by the BBC has found that the drugs – which have been deemed dangerous – are freely available over the counter in shops and sold online by sellers based in the UK and overseas.

SARMs, are a class of drugs that have similar effects to anabolic steroids but are designed to be more selective in their actions. They work to promote muscle growth and bone density and are believed to have worse side effects than steroids in the long term while a full range of effects are yet to be known.

Selling SARMs is a criminal offence in the UK as they are categorised as an 'unauthorised novel food' not used for human consumption and 'should not be consumed', according to the Food Standards Agency (FSA).

BBC said its undercover reporter went to ten shops across the UK and spoke to gym-going young people over the use of muscle-building drugs.

It found that most retailers advised the use of SARMs drugs to build 'bigger and leaner' muscles quickly and sold the products.

A seller in the West Midlands said: 'They're not even strictly for human consumption, but they are effective.' Another recommended against the use of it but sold the product anyway.

The seller, when asked if there were any side effects of the drug, said, 'not really' and mentioned the possibility of lowered testosterone.

'You should be absolutely fine,' he told the BBC reporter.

In a statement, the retailer later said that the staff is well trained in compliance and legality and they 'would never advise anybody to take SARMs. If we get the feeling somebody will be consuming them we immediately refuse the sale'.

FSA said in a statement: 'SARMs are not authorised for sale in the UK and should not be consumed. If consumers become aware of these products on sale, they should report it to the Food Standards Agency or to their local authority.' The Royal Pharmaceutical Society (RPS) is the professional membership body for pharmacists and pharmacies in England, Scotland and Wales calling on the government and regulators to tighten the laws and conduct strict inspections to half their use.

Laura Wilson of the RPS told BBC that side effects range from disrupted hormone levels, liver issues to breast tissue development in men.

'So our advice would be not to take them,' she said.

'We would like to see the laws around them tightened; we would like to see better control over them and an acknowledgment that they are not being used for "research purposes" when they're being purchased.'

7 July 2023

The above information is reprinted with kind permission from *The Independent*.
© independent.co.uk 2024

www.independent.co.uk

Gang jailed for drugs smuggling through the UK and Ireland

Four men who smuggled drugs from the Netherlands to the UK and Ireland have been sentenced to a total of more than 53 years in prison after a National Crime Agency (NCA) investigation.

Anthony Terry, 49, from Wolverhampton, was head of the organised crime group, orchestrating an importation of £1.6 million of cocaine from the Netherlands to England, and then across by ferry to Northern Ireland.

NCA officers seized the drugs, which had been hidden in fuel tanks transported within a van, when it arrived at Belfast port in February 2021. At the same time Terry was under surveillance in Wolverhampton, and he was arrested the same day.

Terry was working with Michael Collis, 63, also from Wolverhampton, who acted as his driver picking up the drugs in the Netherlands.

Two other drivers, Joshpal Singh Kothiria, 34, from Wolverhampton, and Mohammed Omar Khan, 39, from Birmingham, were used to supply the drugs to customers in the UK or export them to the Republic of Ireland.

The group used encrypted messaging service EncroChat to communicate and the NCA was able to identify other occasions in 2020 where Terry had smuggled drugs and cash for other organised crime groups.

Terry instructed Collis to travel to the Netherlands on 6 April 2020 and he collected 17.5 kilos of cocaine. From there, the drugs were divided up and, while Khan made deliveries to Luton and Slough, Collis travelled to the Republic of Ireland to hand over the remaining amount in County Wicklow.

At the same time, Terry sent Kothiria to East London to collect 10 kilos of cannabis and a vacuum-packing machine. Kothiria brought these back to the West Midlands where the cannabis was packed before he took it to County Leitrim in the Republic of Ireland.

A couple of weeks later, Collis picked up 18 kilos of cocaine in the Netherlands, going on to deliver 10 kilos to dealers in the UK before taking the rest to Ireland.

The final drug run captured on EncroChat occurred between 26 May and 3 June 2020, where Terry discussed a cannabis delivery. Kothiria was sent to pick up the load from Leicestershire and take it to the Republic of Ireland.

The drugs were transported to Northern Ireland by ferry before being driven across the country to be dropped off in Ireland. NCA officers worked closely with the Police Service of Northern Ireland and An Garda Síochána in the Republic to track Kothiria's movements.

Later in June 2020, the NCA's Operation Venetic saw the takedown of the Encrochat platform.

Terry and Collis continued their criminality, however, and NCA investigators established that Collis had travelled to the Hook of Holland again in July and September 2020 before returning to England and travelling onwards to Belfast. He then distributed the drugs in Limerick in the Republic of Ireland.

Terry and Collis both pleaded guilty to drug trafficking offences in April 2023. Kothiria and Khan were convicted in May 2023 following a trial at Wolverhampton Crown Court.

They were sentenced at the same court today. Terry was already serving an 18 year sentence in relation to the cocaine seized in Belfast in February 2021.

NCA Branch Commander Mick Pope said: 'These criminals were determined to smuggle drugs into the UK and onwards to the Republic of Ireland. They did not care about the geography of their crimes when in pursuit of pure profit.

'They used the road and ferry networks to take their drugs across the Irish Sea, hoping to avoid detection by taking advantage of the common travel area and border between Northern Ireland and the Republic.'

'This case demonstrates perfectly how the NCA works with partners to tackle cross-border threats between the UK and Ireland, and we will continue do all we can to disrupt and dismantle organised crime groups impacting on local communities.'

8 December 2023

The above information is reprinted with kind permission from the National Crime Agency.
© Crown Copyright 2024
This information is licensed under the Open Government Licence v3.0
To view this licence, visit http://www.nationalarchives.gov.uk/doc/open-government-licence/

www.gov.uk

Chapter 3: Safety and Support

Tips for supporting someone with drug and alcohol problems

Tips to help someone with their drug and alcohol use, including how to look after yourself.

Tips for supporting someone with drug and alcohol problems

It can feel difficult to support someone who is struggling with recreational drug or alcohol use. It might make you feel worried, frustrated, or lonely. But there are things you can do to help.

This might include encouraging them to seek help for the first time. If you are supporting someone seeking help for the first time, you could:

- Reassure them that it is OK to seek help.
- Help them find out what services are available locally. Turning Point's website has a tool to help you find local services for drug and alcohol use.
- Go to appointments with them, if they would like you to. This may especially help for their first visit.

If they already receive treatment or support, you could help them stick to their treatment plan, go to appointments, and meet their targets.

As well as helping them find treatment and support, these are some ways to help someone feel supported:

- Find ways to spend more time together. You could try joining in with any activities that they enjoy.
- Listen to them if they want to talk about their experiences or how they feel.
- Try to explain how their alcohol or drug use is affecting you.

If you are a parent concerned about your child's drug use, the charity Adfam has information for parents supporting children who use recreational drugs.

Can I section someone for drug or alcohol use?

Doctors cannot section someone just because they are addicted to drugs or alcohol.

But if someone who takes drugs or alcohol also has mental health problems, doctors may be able to section them. This is usually only for a mental health emergency, for example if their safety is at risk.

If you are someone's nearest relative, you may be able to ask for them to have a mental health assessment.

Sometimes it's the people looking after others who need care and understanding themselves.

Looking after yourself

Supporting someone else can have a big impact on your own life. By looking after yourself, you might also find it easier to offer support to others.

These are some things you can do to help yourself:

- Talk to someone you trust. It can help to discuss how you feel with someone you trust, such as a friend, family member, or counsellor. Join a support group. This might be something you attend in person or online. Or you might be able to call a helpline, to speak to someone over the phone.
- Try self-care. This could be finding new ways to relax, be creative, or spending time in nature. Or it could be taking care of your physical health, or finding ways to improve your sleep.
- If you care for someone with a dual diagnosis of mental health and drug or alcohol problems, you should be able to have a carer's assessment. This may help you get more practical support with your caring responsibilities.

June 2022

The above information is reprinted with kind permission from Mind.
© 2024 Mind

www.mind.org.uk

Peer mentor programmes could become a pathway out of addiction

The government has developed a £3.7 million peer mentor and employment programme for people with substance dependence to seek help from those who have beat addiction.

Peer mentors with experiences and histories of drug or alcohol dependency are to guide people on a journey away from addiction and into work in a new trial being tested across England.

As many mentors note returning to work being a vital step in their own recovery from addiction, they aim to draw on their lived experiences of drug or alcohol dependency to support people in the same position.

The peer mentor programme is being trialled in 40 Jobcentres as part of efforts by the Department for Work and Pensions (DWP) to help those with substance issues and to grow the economy.

What have peer mentors said about the programme so far?

A peer mentor called Declan, who overcame 20 years of substance dependency thanks to getting help and returning to work, said: 'I spent around 20 years using continuously, almost every couple of days in the second decade. Having a close friend pass away because of an overdose was the beginning of my journey out of substance dependency,

'Volunteering really helped me in my recovery and set me up for a return to work. In my new role as peer mentor, I'm looking forward to helping people who are going through the same sort of issues I had and starting them on their journey to recovery.'

> *'I'm looking forward to helping people who are going through the same sort of issues I had and starting them on their journey to recovery.'* – Declan, Peer Mentor

Gary, another mentor who is drawing from his own experience of opiate dependency in his new role, said: 'I was opiate dependent for 15 years and used crack cocaine. After a short spell in prison, due to offending related to my drug use, I linked with a support worker upon release,

'They pointed me towards a place that supported recovery and helped people gain life and employment skills,

'I'm now pleased to be taking up this new peer mentoring role and helping others who share similar experiences to my own. The space and time DWP are providing for people with drug or alcohol dependency is a vital step in the right direction for their recovery and eventual employment.'

Peer mentors will help those who have applied by disclosing their dependency issues without fear of reprisal.

Signposting people to help, mentors will assist them to manage their addiction, and eventually equip them with the necessary skills to access education, training, volunteering, and employment.

£39 million to support drug and alcohol dependency programmes.

The DWP is also to invest over £39 million in expanding its Individual Placement and Support for drug and alcohol dependency programmes.

Set to be delivered to all local authority areas in England by 2025, this programme will support individuals in structured drug and alcohol treatment to find and remain in employment.

What areas are to see new peer mentoring services open in Jobcentres?

- North East: Hull
- South East: Portsmouth, Cosham, Fareham, Havant, Gosport
- London and Essex: Tower Hamlets, Hackney, Westminster, Camden, Newham, Islington, Croydon, Lambeth
- North West: Liverpool City, Knowsley, Wirral, St Helens, Southport, Sefton, Halton.

Supporting recovery and helping people gain life and employment skills

Minister for Social Mobility, Youth, and Progression, Mims Davies MP, said: 'Our new peer mentors are proof that work can be a crucial part of someone's journey out of substance dependency, transforming their life,

'Their lived experience will help them provide expert one-to-one advice and support from DWP in our Jobcentres, helping people recovering from addiction move into work,

'This new form of support will not only give people in recovery the tailored help they need to get on in life and prosper, but it will also help grow our economy by getting more people back into the workforce.'

23 May 2023

The above information is reprinted with kind permission from Open Access Government.
© 2024 ADJACENT DIGITAL POLITICS LTD

www.openaccessgovernment.org

MPs call for magic mushrooms and psychedelic drugs to be downgraded

Cross-party committee also backs wider use of cannabis for medicinal use and drug 'consumption rooms'.

By Adam Forrest

Magic mushrooms and other psychedelic drugs should be reclassified as 'a matter of urgency' to support clinical research into medical and therapeutic treatment, a group of influential MPs have said.

A report by the home affairs committee said there was a 'growing body of evidence' that suggests psychedelics – and psilocybin in particular – may have therapeutic benefits, including treating depression and post-traumatic stress disorder (PTSD).

The cross-party group recommended that Rishi Sunak's government downgrades the class A psychedelic drugs from schedule 1 to schedule 2 so academics can test the 'therapeutic value' more easily.

The powerful committee backed greater provision of cannabis-based products for medicinal use – though it stopped short of saying cannabis should be legalised or regulated for non-medical use.

The cross-party group of MPs also recommended the use of safe spaces across the UK for users to take heroin and other substances in 'consumption rooms' under medical supervision – along with greater testing at festivals.

The Scottish government has been pressing for a so-called safe consumption facility to be set up, with efforts on this having so far been blocked by Westminster.

But the Home Affairs Committee recommended that a pilot in Glasgow is supported by Westminster and jointly funded by both governments.

If Rishi Sunak's government remains unwilling to support the pilot, the power to establish it should be devolved to the Scottish government, the committee said.

More widely, the MPs recommended pilots of such facilities – where heroin users and other addicts can take substances under medical supervision with the aim that the environment will help prevent overdoses – in parts of the UK where local government deem there is a need.

Figures published last week revealed Scotland's largest ever fall in drug deaths, with data showing a total of 1,051 deaths due to drug misuse in 2022 – a drop of 279 on the previous year.

But while the number of deaths linked to drugs misuse is now at the lowest it has been since 2017, the official report made clear that the rate of deaths is still 'much higher' than it was when recording the data began in 1996.

MPs said the pilot on the bold move 'must be evaluated in order to establish a reliable evidence base on the utility of a safe consumption facility in the UK.'

Responding to the recommendation on consumption rooms, the Sunak government insisted 'there is no safe way to take illegal drugs' and they have 'no plans to consider' the idea.

Additionally, the MPs said on-site drug checking services at temporary events like music festivals and within the night-time economy should be rolled out, recommending that the Home Office 'establish a dedicated licensing scheme for drug checking at such events before the start of the summer 2024 festival season'.

The report stated that existing classifications of controlled substances should be reviewed by the Advisory Council on the Misuse of Drugs (ACMD) to ensure they accurately reflect the risk of harm, with further reviews every 10 years.

While welcoming the 10-year drug strategy's commitment to tackling county lines, the committee said the government can 'go further to prevent children and young people from becoming exploited'.

Committee chairwoman, Dame Diana Johnson said: 'The criminal justice system will need to continue to do all it can to break up the criminal gangs that drive the trade in illicit drugs. However, it must also recognise that many children and young people involved need to be supported to escape, not punished for their involvement.'

She added: 'Fundamentally, we need to have the right interventions in place to help people break free from the terrible cycles of addiction and criminality that drug addiction can cause. Simply attempting to remove drugs from people's lives hasn't worked.'

The Association of Police and Crime Commissioners (APCC) said many commissioners |will not, however, feel that they can support approaches that they see as facilitating illegal drug use, such as drug consumption rooms and pill testing, and they therefore support the current legal position.'

31 August 2023

The above information is reprinted with kind permission from *The Independent*.
© independent.co.uk 2024

www.independent.co.uk

'Drug use is a health problem': inside one of the world's oldest legal consumption rooms

At Quai 9 in Geneva, safe equipment and healthcare have cut overdoses and illnesses among addicts. But around the world, opinion is divided on whether such projects really work.

By Charlotte Lytton

In a lime-green room behind Geneva's main train station, a man is slumped over a chair, the heroin he has just injected taking effect. Around him, a handful of others are in the process of reaching that same state of bliss: administering bands to their arms to produce a vein, unpeeling plastic-clad syringes, exhaling as the needle goes in. Some will return later today – maybe a handful of times – to get their hit at one of the oldest supervised drug consumption rooms in the world, where users can take their own illicit substances without fear of prosecution.

A state-provided supply of safe injecting equipment, along with tea, croissants, and hot showers, may seem an unusual way to handle a citywide drug epidemic, but Geneva's Quai 9 facility – which turned 20 this year – may well provide a blueprint for Britain. In September 2023, it was announced that the UK's first legal consumption room is to open in Glasgow, a city in a country with higher fatal overdose rates than anywhere in Europe; deaths caused by drug poisoning in Scotland are 2.7 times higher than the UK average. First proposed seven years ago, the site – five minutes from the city centre's main drag, by a Morrison's and a pram shop – will cost £7 million to build.

Kirsten Horsburgh, Chief Executive of the Scottish Drugs Forum, says she is 'delighted' by this 'massive, massive achievement over many years' for health leaders and city officials in Glasgow, 'who should be applauded for their tenacity and resilience in trying to push this forward.'

Studies of the approximately 120 facilities worldwide appear positive: Vancouver's has been 'associated with improved health outcomes' such as reducing HIV and hepatitis C transmission by providing clean needles; Sydney's, which opened in 2001, noted a reduction in ambulance callouts. A 2011 paper found that consumption rooms reduced fatal overdose rates by a third, while a paper published by French researchers last year showed that emergency department visits and crime dropped once they had been introduced, too.

Its proponents argue that consumption rooms not only provide better outcomes for users' health, but for the public – and the public purse. Reduced illnesses and overdoses means fewer people needing medical care; a 2021 government review found that the societal cost of drug misuse in England and Wales is £20 billion annually, yet that for every £1 spent on harm reduction and treatment, there is a fourfold return on investment via alleviated pressure on health and justice services.

'It's really hard to find people who are against drug consumption rooms,' Horsburgh says, adding that if one were to open close to her home, she would 'welcome it.'

Of course, not everyone is on side. The idea seems mind-boggling to many, even if consumption rooms have been around for close to four decades (the first opened in Bern, Switzerland, in 1986). After a five-year trial, a small group of vocal protesters expressed their fury at the recent opening of the medically supervised injecting room (MSIR) in Melbourne, sharing photos of addicts lying in the street outside in a chemically induced stupor. (Its location, next to a primary school, has been a key source of ire.)

Horsburgh appreciates that 'there's always the mystique around these types of services. If you've never been familiar with them before, if you've never visited a facility like this, it's really difficult to understand how it operates, what it does, what outcomes can be for people.' As such, she thinks the most important next step for Glasgow – along with ensuring the facility doesn't enter a protracted consultation period that derails it from its opening, projected to be within a matter of months – is a 'really good consultation with the neighbours, because while a lot of people may be supportive of services for people who use drugs, quite often it's then the "well, not in my back yard" stuff.'

Quai 9 appeared to have cracked that. Run by Première Ligne (a nonprofit focusing on drug harm reduction), with 4m Swiss francs (about £3.6m) in funding from the Canton of Geneva over the past year, it has become a fundamental part of the city's makeup. Its central location (considered a necessity for consumption rooms, so they are based where excessive drug use is) and lurid lime-green exterior are not intended to hide its identity, but signpost it to those in need – something that requires close cooperation between local businesses and residents, police, healthcare, and housing facilities. It is seen as mutually beneficial: reducing the number of addicts who would otherwise have been consuming drugs on the street or on doorsteps, potentially in large groups, and leaving drug paraphernalia on the floor.

The relationship between the centre and locals, and the fact that, to date, there has not been a lethal overdose at Quai 9, are 'a matter of pride… It's nice to think that good decisions were taken in Geneva', says Ruth Dreifuss, a former Swiss president and ex-chair of the Global Commission on Drug Policy (which includes a handful of world leaders, Richard Branson, and Nick Clegg).

Dreifuss, who was elected to the Swiss cabinet in the early 1990s – when the country was in the grip of the HIV crisis

– is adamant that 'drug use is a health problem,' and that the 'illusion' that it is a social ill that can be dealt with by 'repressive' criminal laws alone 'really has to stop, and to be replaced by pragmatic answers to the needs of the people who use drugs.' She believes that penalising users of illicit substances serves only to potentially worsen their health and social footing when they are forced through the justice system for something that could be overseen safely.

Yet in recent months, Quai 9 has been hit hard by new challenges. Geneva, along with other cities in Switzerland, is facing a crack cocaine epidemic, with cheap 'rocks' available for as little as £9. Its presence on the streets has become so strong that Quai 9 has introduced a smoking room in its facility, with plastic dividers to help contain the fumes. 'You cannot predict what's going to be the next step,' says Thomas Herquel, Première Ligne's Director. 'The only thing I know is that I don't know.'

> **'We think sometimes that the only path is to have some kind of authoritarian response'** – Dr Nico Clark, Head of Addiction Medicine, Royal Melbourne Hospital

Around the world, shifting drug use habits have unseated what appeared to be permissive drug law success stories. Portugal decriminalised consumption of all drugs for personal use in 2001; it technically remains against the law, but instead of prison, users are registered by police and referred for help (attendance is voluntary). In the early days, it appeared to be an unequivocal success: HIV transmission rates via syringes dropped, as did the number of overdoses, and prison populations were down 16.5% by 2008. But a recent national survey shows illicit drug use went up from 7.8% to 12.8% between 2001 and 2022; overdose rates are at a 12-year high, having nearly doubled in Lisbon between 2019 and 2023 (this is still below the European average). In Porto, there has been a 24% jump in drug paraphernalia being collected from city streets in the year to 2022, with this year set to outpace that. Crimes such as robbery in public spaces rose 14% from 2021 to 2022, which police have in part blamed on the rise in drug use.

Drug reforms in Oregon and Canada have also failed to live up to their promises. Measure 110, introduced in the US state three years ago to limit the role of law enforcement in drug use, has resulted in rising overdoses and delays in funding for treatment; a statewide non-partisan poll in May 2023 found that more than 60% of residents believe the policy has worsened levels of addiction, crime, and homelessness. In British Columbia, decriminalisation efforts amid an opioid crisis have been called a 'failed experiment' by the Conservative party leader, Pierre Poilievre.

Dr Nico Clark led the establishment of the MSIR in Melbourne, worked on drug treatment efforts at the World Health Organization, and is now Head of Addiction Medicine at Royal Melbourne hospital. He remains optimistic that 'if you redesign [drug] services in a way that works for [drug users], then you have this combined benefit of helping people stay alive, but also helping them change their lives and improve their lives.' He points to figures showing a drop in ambulance callouts in the area around the centre once it opened, and data modelling that estimates more than 6,000 overdoses have since been successfully managed, and 63 lives saved.

Its location next to a community health centre has, he says, made it possible to give further treatment quickly, including dental services for those whose drug use had severely damaged their teeth, as 'not only does it cause chronic pain, but it severely limits their opportunity to re-engage with society… We had so many examples of people who transformed their lives before our eyes.' Opposition, he adds, is based less on centres' efficacy, more on the 'huge stigma' that drug-taking retains. 'It's confronting for us as a society… we think sometimes the only path is to have some kind of authoritarian response or take [drug users] away.'

For Keith Humphreys, a professor of psychiatry and behavioural sciences at Stanford University, it is hard to conclude whether consumption rooms – which 'have become a battleground in the culture wars' – are really the answer to rising global drug use rates.

Evidence to date is 'methodologically weak'. Humphreys says. 'Supervised drug consumption sites may make a small difference or they may not, especially when compared with better evidenced services [such as treatment with medications and counselling, or provision of naloxone, used to reverse the effects of an opioid overdose] that could be supported with the same money.'

Increasingly, how well consumption rooms work comes down to what 'working' looks like. Do reduced ambulance callouts and less antisocial behaviour constitute success? Or does that only come with a drop in drug use and crime rates? Is the main goal simply keeping people who would be injecting anyway off the streets?

Vincent*, who has been visiting Quai 9 for six years, is that dichotomy made flesh. 'At the beginning I was only smoking heroin. After four or five months, I started injecting, and started mixing medication [taking other substances], which made things feel much stronger,' he tells me. 'It makes me calm, but at the same time, it's a false calm, because I'm very nervous, stressed, and anxious.' Inside his mind is a prison, he says, from which he is unable to escape.

He is grateful for the centre, to 'have a safe place to smoke and inject; we don't have to use drugs outside people's houses, [or] on the streets.' But he also attends five times a day, his addiction showing no signs of slowing. Vincent aspires to have 'a beautiful family,' he says, smiling; 'to be given a chance.' Quai 9 may be the safest place he can achieve that. But there is no guarantee.

*Name has been changed

3 December 2023

Debate

As a class, debate legal consumption rooms. Half of the class will be for and the other half against.

The above information is reprinted with kind permission from *The Guardian*.
© 2024 Guardian News and Media Limited

www.theguardian.com

Feeling pressured to take drugs? Here are 10 ways to deal with it

1. Remember that you're not alone. It's easy to think you're the only one who's not tried drugs but, actually, most young people don't take drugs.
2. Work out where you stand on issues like sex, drugs, and alcohol. Knowing your own mind makes it easier to stay true to yourself.
3. Prepare yourself. Think about how you'd like to respond when someone offers you drugs so you know what to say.
4. Try to understand who's offering you the drugs and why. Friends should understand if you say no; people you don't know you very well may expect something in return.
5. Say no firmly but clearly and without making a big deal about it. If they try to persuade you, don't feel like you have to change your mind.
6. Remember that, although they may not show it, your mates will respect you more if you're assertive and clear about what you do and don't want to do.
7. Take a look around. You'll soon see that you're not the only one worrying about what other people think of you. Try to focus on your own opinion of yourself – in the end, that's all that matters.
8. Worried about your mates being pressured? Don't keep it to yourself: talk to them, or someone you trust.
9. If you're finding it hard to be yourself within your group, take a step back, and think about whether it's time to find a new crowd to hang out with.
10. Before trying anything new it makes sense to know what's what. You can find out more about different drugs on the Drugs A to Z on the Talk to Frank website, or call FRANK on 0300 123 6600 at any time, day or night.

The above information is reprinted with kind permission from Department of Health & Social Care.
© Crown Copyright 2023
This information is licensed under the Open Government Licence v3.0
To view this licence, visit http://www.nationalarchives.gov.uk/doc/open-government-licence/

OGL

www.talktofrank.com

Spiking – how to protect yourself on a night out

What does spiking mean?

To spike a drink means to put alcohol or drugs into someone's drink without their knowledge or permission. This might be with the intention to incapacitate someone enough to rob or even sexually assault them. Although sometimes spiking can be intended as a joke, it's a very bad joke that is both dangerous and illegal.

There is also some concern at the possibility that people are being 'spiked' by needles/syringes containing drugs. Although this is much less likely than drink spiking, a lot of the advice for staying safe from spiking a drink can also protect you from the possibility of needle spiking too. Spiking is a criminal offence and whilst all venues should be taking steps to ensure they are safe places to be, you may still need to protect yourself, particularly if you feel at risk or you're in a place that is unfamiliar.

How to stay safe

- Plan your night out, including your journey there and back.
- Make sure the venue you are going to is licenced – venues are required to take steps to ensure the safety of their customers.
- When going to a pub, club, or party, avoid going alone. Friends can look out for one another.
- Be aware of what's going on around you and keep away from situations you don't feel comfortable with.
- Think very carefully about whether you should leave a pub, club, or party with someone you've just met.
- Make sure your mobile phone has plenty of charge in it before you leave home and keep your mobile safe and accessible.

How to avoid drink spiking

- Always buy your own drink and watch it being poured.
- Don't accept drinks from strangers.
- Never leave your drink unattended while you dance or go to the toilet.
- Don't drink or taste anyone else's drink.
- Throw your drink away if you think it tastes strange or different.

What to do if you think you've been spiked (by drink or needle)

- If you start to feel strange, sick, or drunk when you know that you couldn't be drunk, get help from a trusted friend or the venue management.
- If you think you may have been spiked, ask a close friend to get you out of the venue or party as soon as possible and either take you home or to hospital (if seriously unwell).
- You could also ring a friend, relative, or partner and ask them to come and pick you up.
- If you feel unsafe, vulnerable, or threatened you can ask for help by approaching venue staff and asking for 'Angela'. This is a coded-phrase that indicates you need help and a trained member of staff will support and assist you. You can also ask for 'Angela' if you are in any situation where you feel threatened or at risk.
- Make sure you can trust the person you ask for help. Don't go anywhere with a stranger or someone you don't know very well.
- Once you are safely home, ask someone to stay with you until the effects of the drug have worn off - this might take several hours.
- Don't hesitate to call for medical help if you need it - it's always better to get checked out.
- Tell the police what has happened as soon as you can - we know it can be scary to do this but the police are there to help you and will listen. Call 999 or 101 – the police need to know as much as they can about spiking so they can help to stop this happening in the future.
- If you have been sexually assaulted, you can contact a sexual assault referral centre for support – find your nearest centre on the NHS website.

The law

The Sexual Offences Act 2003 states that it is an offence to administer a substance, to a person with intent to overpower that person to enable sexual activity with them. It is punishable by up to ten years imprisonment. This means that slipping alcohol or drugs into someone's drink is against the law, even if the drink is not consumed or the person is not harmed. The same would be true of needle spiking, which would also be a physical assault.

If you've been affected by crime and you need confidential support or information, you can also call Victim Support on 0808 168 9111.

The above information is reprinted with kind permission from Department of Health & Social Care.
© Crown Copyright 2023
This information is licensed under the Open Government Licence v3.0
To view this licence, visit http://www.nationalarchives.gov.uk/doc/open-government-licence/

www.talktofrank.com

Further Reading/ Useful Websites

Useful websites

www.blogs.lse.ac.uk

www.drugwise.org.uk

www.economicsobservatory.com

www.gov.uk

www.independent.co.uk

www.metro.co.uk

www.mind.org.uk

www.openaccessgovernment.org

www.talktofrank.com

www.telegraph.co.uk

www.theconversation.com

www.theguardian.com

www.ukat.co.uk

www.YouGov.co.uk

Further Reading

References p14-15:

1. WHO (2019). *International Classification of Diseases for Mortality and Morbidity Statistics*. Eleventh Revision.

2. UNODC (2021). *World Drug Report 2021*. Available at: https://www.unodc.org/unodc/data-and-analysis/wdr2021.html

3. CDC WONDER (2020). National Centre on Health Statistics

4. CDC Emergency Preparedness and Response: Increase in Fatal Drug Overdoses Across the United States Driven by Synthetic Opioids Before and During the COVID-19 Pandemic, 17 December 2020. Available at: https://emergency.cdc.gov/han/2020/han00438.asp

5. Degenhardt L, Glantz M, Evans-Lacko S, et al. (2017). *Estimating treatment coverage for people with substance use disorders: an analysis of data from the World Mental Health Surveys*. World Psychiatry. 2017;16(3):299-307. doi:10.1002/wps.2045

6. https://www.ncbi.nlm.nih.gov/pmc/articles/PMC7388229/

7. https://www.health.harvard.edu/blog/access-to-medical-marijuana-reduces-opioid-prescriptions-2018050914509

Where can I find help?

Below are some telephone numbers, email addresses, and websites of agencies or charities that can offer support or advice if you, or someone you know, needs it.

Talk to Frank
Helpline: 0300 123 6600
www.talktofrank.com

Childline
Helpline: 0800 1111
www.childline.org.uk

Action on Addiction
www.actiononaddiction.org.uk

Re-solv
Helpline: 01785 817885
www.re-solv.org

Scottish Families Affected by Alcohol & Drugs
Helpline: 08080 10 10 11
www.sfad.org.uk

The Wales Drug And Alcohol Helpline
Helpline: 0808 808 2234 (24/7)
www.dan247.org.uk

Drug Addicts Anonymous
Helpline: 0300 030 3000
www.drugaddictsanonymous.org.uk

Narcotics Anonymous UK
Helpline: 0300 999 1212 (10am - midnight)
www.ukna.org

NHS
www.nhs.uk
Non-emergency helpline: 111

Remember, you can always speak to your GP, or a trusted adult.

If you are in danger and need immediate help, please call 999.

Glossary

Addiction
A dependence on a substance which makes it very difficult to stop taking it. Addiction can be either physical, meaning the user's body has become dependent on the substance and will suffer negative symptoms if the substance is withdrawn, or psychological, meaning a user has no physical need to take a substance, but will experience strong cravings if it is withdrawn.

Amphetamines
Synthetic drugs which can be swallowed, inhaled, or injected. Their effects can include increased mental alertness, energy, and confidence. Most amphetamines are Class B substances, but crystal meth and prepared-for-injection speed are Class A. Taking amphetamines can cause anxiety or paranoia and risks include overdose and psychological dependence. They can also put strain on a user's heart, leading to cardiac problems.

Cannabinoids
Cannabinoids are chemicals found in the cannabis plant. Synthetic cannabinoids are a group of substances that mimic the effects of tetrahydrocannabinol(THC), which is the substance that is primarily responsible for the major psychoactive effects of cannabis. imited information is available about how these substances work and their toxic effects in humans.

Cannabis
Cannabis is the most widely used illegal drug in Britain. Made from parts of the cannabis plant, it's a naturally occurring drug. It is a mild sedative (often causing a chilled-out feeling or actual sleepiness) and it's also a mild hallucinogen (meaning users may experience a state where they see objects and reality in a distorted way and may even hallucinate). The main active compound in cannabis is tetrahydrocannabinol (THC). Slang names include dope, ganja, grass, hash, marijuana, weed and pot.

Detox
Ridding the body of toxins, i.e. drugs.

Drug
A chemical that alters the way the mind and body works. Legal drugs include alcohol, tobacco, caffeine and prescription medicines taken for medical reasons. Illegal drugs taken for recreation include cannabis, cocaine, ecstasy and speed. These illegal substances are divided into three classes – A, B, and C – according to the danger they pose to the user and to society (with A being the most harmful and C the least).

Drug driving law
In the UK it is illegal to drive if you are unfit to do so because you are taking legal or illegal drugs, or if you have certain levels of illegal drugs in your blood.

Hallucinogen
A drug which produces visions and sensations detached from reality (a 'trip'). Common hallucinogens include LSD, ketamine and magic mushrooms.

Legal high
Also known as psychoactive substances, legal highs function as stimulants and have mood-altering properties. Producing or trading in these substances will became illegal in the UK in 2016.

Misuse of Drugs Act 1971
Legislation prohibiting the use of dangerous recreational substances, making it an offence to possess banned drugs for personal use or with the intent to supply. It also divides drugs into three classes according to the degree of harm they pose to the individual and to society – A, B, or C – each with different associated penalties.

Opiates
Drugs made from the opium poppy, such as heroin, opium and morphine. Methadone is a synthetic opioid: an artificial substance designed to act on the same opioid receptors as morphine and heroin. It is often used to treat people with a dependency on these substances.

Reclassification
When an illegal substance is moved from one drugs class into another, after its harmfulness has been reassessed or new research has uncovered previously unknown negative effects. For example, cannabis was reclassified twice in less than a decade, being moved from Class B to Class C in 2004 and back to Class B again in 2009.

Recreational drug
A drug that is taken occasionally and is often claimed to be non-addictive.

Rehab
A course of treatment for drug or alcohol dependence, typically at a residential facility.

Risky behaviour
Behaviour that has the potential to get out of control or become dangerous.

Solvent
A volatile substance which gives off fumes. Vapours from products including paint, glue and aerosols can be inhaled and cause intoxication. Volatile substance abuse is highly dangerous, killing more children aged ten to 15 than all illegal drugs put together.

Stimulant
A substance that speeds up the nervous system, making people feel more alert or energised (mentally and physically). These drugs are also known as 'uppers' and include caffeine, cocaine, ecstasy, and speed.

THC
THC is an abbreviation of delta-9-tetrahydrocannabinol. This is the main psychoactive ingredient in cannabis and leads to the feeling of being 'stoned.' The higher the concentration of this chemical, the more potent the strain of cannabis. It is because of this ingredient that cannabis is one of the most easily detectable drugs when carrying out drugs tests, as THC can take weeks to clear from the body.

Index

A
addiction 14–15, 20–21
austerity 17, 26
availability 2

B
body, effects on 6–9, 10, 20–21, 22
body building 33

C
cannabis 13, 14, 25, 32, 37
classification of drugs 23, 24–25
consumption rooms 37, 38–39
cost to society 26, 38

D
deaths 16–17, 26
decriminalisation 26–29
depressants 6
discrimination 32
drinking 20–21

E
ecstasy 5
evidence-based policies 26–27, 32
experimentation 1

G
gender 5
government policies 26–27, 32, 37

H
hallucinogens 6
help, getting 23

L
laws 10–11, 23, 41 *see also* decriminalisation
legal drugs 23

M
mental health 9, 35
methods of drug taking 4–5
Misuse of Drugs Act 10, 23

N
new psychoactive substances (NPS) 10–11, 23
nitrous oxide (laughing gas) 22

P
peer mentoring 36
peer pressure 1, 13, 15, 40
penalties 23, 24–25, 28–29, 32
Perry, Matthew 20–21
personal factors (set) 5
Portugal 26, 39
possession 23, 25, 30–31
prescription drugs 1, 18–19
prevalence 11, 12–15
psychoactive substances 10–11, 23, 24–25
Psychoactive Substances Act 10–11, 23
public opinion 26, 28–31

R
reasons for taking drugs 1–2
reclassification 37
recovery 21
recreational drug use 1, 12–15, 32
risks of drug use 4–5

S
SARMs (Selective Androgen Receptor Modulators) 33
Scotland 37, 38
self medication 1
selling 30–31
setting 5
Sexual Offences Act 40
smuggling 34
spiking 41
stimulants 6
support 35–36

T
treatment services 17, 26, 37, 38–39
types of drug 6

W
withdrawal 9